Agile

The Ultimate Guide to Agile Project Management and Kanban for Agile Software Development, Including Explanations for Lean, Scrum, XP, FDD and Crystal

Contents

Part 1: Agile Project Management

How to Make Your Customers Happier While Saving Money, Time, and Effort

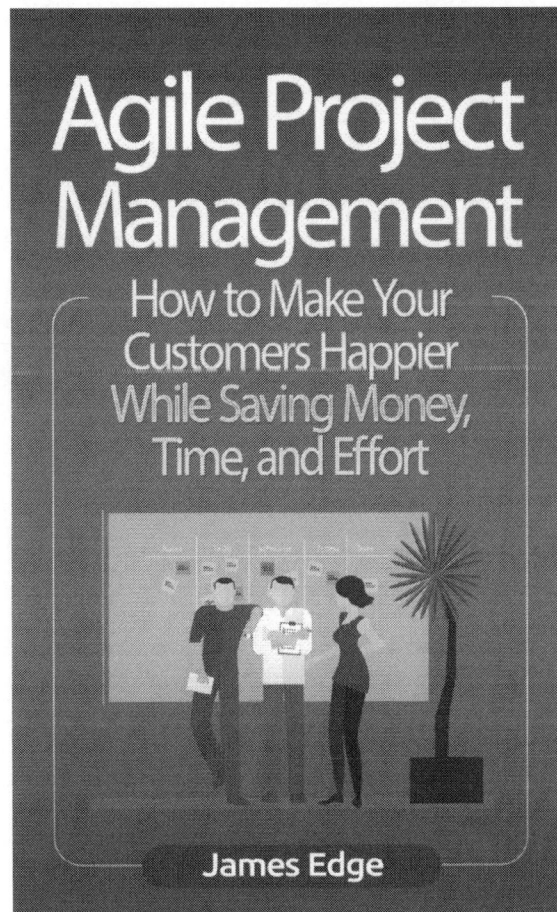

Introduction

The following chapters will walk you through all the details you need to know to successfully implement agile project management into your business for success. Enjoy success in profits, efficiency, and input. To experience this, you must first understand what project management is and why agile is different from more traditional approaches. There are several persuasive reasons why you will want to choose agile over any other option out there, which you will understand after reading Chapter 3. Once you are clear on why this is such a valuable tool, the details of agile are outlined for your implementation.

When you are ready to start implanting agile in your workplace, you need to know what the foundational principles and values are as well, as the way you can test your project to determine if it is a candidate for agile project management. The next step is to learn how to apply these values and principles to your project, including assigning agile roles and environment. Finally, after implementing agile to complete a project, it is important for you to review the results to make sure that it was implemented effectively and where you can adjust for future success. This includes managing quality and risks. After all, the effort you put into planning can provide replicable results in the future, but you want to make sure those results are the most financially and efficiently delivered. So now, get ready to learn all you need to know to guide your business toward happy customers, fuller pockets, more time free on your calendar, and less stress in the effort!

Chapter 1: What is Agile Project Management?

Maybe you tried it a little or just heard rumors about agile project management, but one thing is for sure, you cannot deny that a project manager is a superhero! Your customers expect their outcome within their budget and timeline. But then, the requirements change, again and again. This is such a common occurrence and one of the main reasons you need to consider agile project management over the unforgiving traditional approach. With agile, even with a moving deliverable, you can still provide customers with precise status updates and hit important targets. This is possible because an agile project manager gets consistent feedback, and the process is more visible. They can then respond faster to changes and problems in the process. This means the results are better and quicker.

What Is Agile?

Agile is more than a daily stand-up meeting. You cannot say your team is "agile" until you truly understand what agile is and what roles are required. Accepting change, providing high-quality work, giving current updates, controlling the budget, managing the timeline, and keeping the scope in perspective are all benefits of agile. This is drastically different than the older project management process that can end up being cumbersome, pricey, and prone to error. Previously, project management produced unreliable results, until agile.

Introduced in 1957, agile project management, which is also referred to as iterative project management, lingered until 2001. The Agile Manifesto was released, and agile became a hot topic, especially in the software development world. That's because this manifesto stressed working together and the need for a speedy response to change, which are the two difficult processes in traditional project management. Projects can be debilitated with delays that are long and costly, especially when a customer has waited to put the final touches on the project's expectations before getting your results. Being agile puts you in the driver's seat, able to give your customer what they want when they want it, making you look stellar at the same time!

Instead of approaching a project as one complex entity that has phases to complete before the next begins, agile allows you to break the project into small usable bits to be developed in a few weeks simultaneously, all leading to the final project. The timeline to complete a small portion typically takes no longer than four weeks. Traditional project management is complex, with a lengthy timeline, and is focused solely on the entire project. With agile, you chunk up the project according to the broad ideas and allow the teams to design, create, construct, and assess their part before adding it to the whole. Another difference between agile and traditional is that agile has three roles to handle the responsibility instead of one.

The three roles of agile include:

1. *Product Owner* - Sets project goals, navigates the scope versus the schedule for the trade-off, handles the changes to the requirements of the project, and develops the features of the products priorities.
2. *Scrum Master* - Assists the group with prioritizing tasks, and eliminates challenges that affect their ability to complete their tasks. This is a new role for agile.
3. *Team Members* - Complete tasks assigned to them, manage the details each day, reports on the progress made, and oversee the product quality control.

Concepts you may have also heard about like: Kanban, Lean, and Scrum, are all methods for structured project management that were created from the concept of agile. They each improved it in various ways, but ultimately the foundation from agile is responsible for making them more successful in the completion of their projects.

Why Is Agile Important?

One of the most important parts of agile project management is the ability to scrutinize and adjust. If you have tried agile before and found it too hard, it is possible you were missing this part. When you include this function in your agile, you will notice that every time you deliver a product, it only gets better and better. In addition, you can expect your customers to get better value from your team members' deliverables, and your company can expect the get more value from you.

The process of agile incorporates an evaluation of cost and time, and it considers them the main constraint. To provide quality output and engage in established processes, your team's schedule is committed to giving immediate feedback, developed with the intention of adapting constantly, and a quality assurance protocol. Metrics are proactively delivered in real time to agile project managers through things like "Cumulative Flow," "Burndown," and "Velocity." This is instead of traditional project management's Gantt charts, Excel spreadsheets or ridiculous milestones. These changes are what makes agile important to the success of your business; the faster completion time and fewer mistakes that pop up at the end, the more money it costs you.

The Scalability of Agile

Companies can fall into the trap of finding success with one agile team and then creating more without a clear path for expansion. This common occurrence leads to a mixture of teams working independently with the tools that are not connected to the singular or clear vision of your company. The reason this occurs often is that scaling agile is a difficult task that requires thought and a follow-through. That being said, it can be done more efficiently using a few keys steps. For example, a project manager, who knows from the beginning that one of the major components to their job is balancing delivery with ROI, is paramount to the success of scalability. This means that the project manager must deliver the objectives on time by using a process that consistently operates at the lowest cost while providing the highest ROI. The best way to do this is to have the agile project management work with the Scrum team. This setup allows for an easily repeated process that can be replicated across various projects and teams. Repeating this process is also successful in alternative locations. An agile project management team with Scrum creates a central location for all defects, tests, tasks, requests, and requirements and turns this knowledge into an invaluable tool. The team can now work together and make decisions without wasting time, as well as delivering the stakeholders the information necessary for their needs precisely when it is needed.

The Strengths of Agile

The number one strength for agile project management is the flexibility it offers. You can adapt the process to anything you need. This is one of the reasons it was used at the foundation for other systems, like Lean or Kanban. Boiling down the idea of agile into the concept of chopping up your project into deliverable pieces that can be completed simultaneously, allows you to modify the details to fit what you need.

The second strength of agile is the priority of responsiveness to change, over sticking to the plan. This again plays into the number one strength of flexibility; however, it is a distinct feature that sets agile apart. You can deliver your product continually with a clear path and system to get you there.

The Weaknesses of Agile

As it typically occurs, the greatest strength is also its greatest weakness. Flexibility can result in a lack of attention and motivation to complete your project if you do not watch over it. Having a loose plan instead of milestones means there is no set process to check in on and see that there is a smooth progression. This looseness can result in the team losing focus. To combat this weakness, consider creating an internal process to run alongside agile to help keep your teams on target, or consistently check in to ensure your teams are constantly communicating and moving onward. Sometimes you may even need to consider one of the offshoots of agile if you continue to find this weakness tripping up your teams.

Chapter 2: Agile Project Management vs. Traditional Project Management

As mentioned in the earlier chapter, there is a vast difference between agile project management and traditional project management; however, there are some important overlaps as well. No matter what form of project management a company employs, the purpose is the same: remove unnecessary glitches from the processes of their company. This vital role has made it a staple to the success of many businesses, so they can get their work done. It does not matter if the project management process is a traditional waterfall method or agile, the companies are after the same thing. So, no matter if the project is for managing a workflow or for time frames, the project management tool helps you keep moving forward with minimal disruption.

Despite the beauty of the possibility, there are limitations to the "magic" of project management. There are several approaches to project management, and many support the claim that agile if the most flexible and practical tool available to companies now. Agile is able to support various projects, among many other clear advantages.

Traditional Project Management Overview

Project management can be applied to a variety of fields and projects. It is a global process with simple objectives and concepts. No matter if you are intentionally or unintentionally tackling a project, there is an element of management in it. When you use project management to complete your projects, you are following basic guidelines, no matter the form you choose. Those forms of project management can be broken into the two distinct classifications: traditional and modern, like agile.

When following a traditional approach, you are choosing a more conventional process and time-tested techniques. This approach can be applied to almost any field or project and has evolved over several decades. According to PMBOK, or Project Management Body of Knowledge, the standard definition for traditional project management is, "a set of techniques and tools that can be applied to an activity that seeks an end product, outcomes or a service." There is a plethora of different definitions offered online, but the basics all boil back down to this standard definition provided by PMBOK.

Agile Overview

Flexibility, collaboration with the customer, and teamwork is the focus of agile, compared to the prominence of time, scope, and cost associated with the preplanning process for traditional project management. The agile process dives into the changes that naturally occur and observes the effort from the group, so the customer receives results and not just an outline of a preplanned process. Project managers who have worked in the field for a long time, enjoy the planning that can be adapted to various scenarios and easy changes, so they love working with agile.

The off-shoots of agile include Kanban and Scrum. These are the two most commonly referenced by companies and professionals. Scrum has a reputation for encouraging the process of making a decision and discouraging wasting time on things that will most likely change anyway. The most important outcome for an agile process is the satisfaction of a client. Providing the project on or ahead of schedule is one way agile can definitely accomplish that outcome.

Traditional vs. Agile Comparison

Traditional or Other Approach	Agile
Managers control change	Teams are responsive and adaptable to changes
Process plans are the most important element	The customer's satisfaction and needs are the most important elements
The hierarchy is strictly top-down, making the teams have to run all decisions through the manager and creating a lag in production time	Teams are self-manageable and self-sufficient; they can make quick decisions for the best of their piece as well as the overall project
Plans are created in the beginning and carried throughout the life of the project, despite changes	An evolution of the process occurs over time and speeds up as it further develops
Irrelevant metrics are ignored	The customer's delivered value is the most important measurable metric
Not inclusive or customizable	Profoundly customizable and inclusive

How Can Agile Work with Other Project Management Processes?

Several project managers have asked this question; the answer is not straightforward, however. This is because agile can work with other processes, but it needs to be done cautiously and on different projects. Having two project management groups approach the same task in their own, unique ways is not effective for many reasons — including financial and interpersonal. People working against one another like that will result in animosity rather than customer value. In addition, implementing two strategies together, such as agile and waterfall, could result in one canceling the other out or realizing that it is not the most effective approach. Still, it is possible.

Despite the above-mentioned suggestions for combining agile with another process, it is also fair to explore the ideas of those opposed to the concept. The primary reason people do not believe agile could work with another method is because of the differences between the two. In addition, the combination can cause confusion in your company and derail the progress of the project.

The Reasons Agile is Favored

There are several reasons that project managers prefer agile to other forms of project management. Some of those reasons include the divisible sections, the internal organizational structure, and the engagement of the customer.

Divisible Sections

"Iterations" is the term assigned to the various sections a project is divided into. After one iteration is completed, it is then immediately sent to the customer. As each is sent to the customer, they can see if the project will be successful or can adjust as needed along the way. This method also allows you the freedom not to preplan the entire project.

Internal Organizational Structure

Management runs parallel to the project's iterations. Groups are managed to complete a piece of the overall project, instead of having one dominant supervisor who oversees all the employees. Often in an agile company, there can be several groups working on a specific project. Each one of the groups has an internal manager who is not guided by external pressure. Interactions between the teams only occur to discuss the project and link processes if one team lacks the ability to complete a task internally.

Most agile projects have three components:

1. Owner - This person is the expert for the overall project and the central point of contact and review for all the teams.
2. Scrum Master - The agile process is overseen by this role. They check in with each iteration along the way and make sure it is completed.
3. Team - The critical component to the success of each iteration, is the group of employees working to complete the tasks. There are both large and small roles within a team, but they are all significant to the process of the project.

Engagement of the Customer

Engaging your customer is the primary concern in an agile environment. As an iteration is completed and sent to the customer, the customer is responsible for giving feedback to the owner, which the team then needs to act upon.

When you compare agile to the more traditional systems, it is obvious agile is superior. The comparison here highlights the features of agile and why it is considered one of the top project management systems worldwide.

Chapter 3: Reasons to be Agile

The beauty and the pain of project management is that it looks idyllic on paper, with its "practical" applications and defined practices, but the application begins to reveal the pain of implementation. If you do not spend the time learning agile, or any project management for that matter, and try to implement practices too quickly, you will find things to be ineffective and unbalanced. Your project will suffer from unequal risk, quality, cost, time, and scope. You and your company's culture need to be structured and prepared before taking this method on. This is why you will find those who praise agile and those who vehemently oppose it.

To make agile work for you and your company, you need to approach it as a tool that will help you run your organization; it is not your organization that should be run by agile. Instead, it is important you discover how you can implement this agile tool into your company's structure and values system so that it complements the overarching mission of your company.

Adapting to agile:

1. Philosophize on the concept until the process engineers are not able to objectively develop the project.
2. Shift focus from the end goal to the process each time so that it becomes a habit.

Of course, there are more approaches within these two extreme examples, the reasons you should consider agile for your company, and the methods you can take to successfully adopt it.

The History of Agile

Since it became mainstream, agile has passed through its own waves of application and adaptation. In the beginning, it gained notoriety for its ability to help a software company get their product to market faster than using a traditional project management approach. This was termed "MVP" or "Minimum Viable Product." Now small or medium-sized companies had an implemented model to help them get more result for less time, money, etc. When these little businesses showed success with this model, larger organizations wanted to jump on board. They saw the benefit of better customer interaction and products getting to market faster.

As companies tweaked and adapted the early agile to their businesses, another phase of agile was created. This phase involved the businesses that did not adopt the previous methods but wanted to capitalize on the benefits. The reason this was a distinct wave in the development of agile is that these late adopters had uncertain motivations. Also, they were more invested in the outcomes, as with traditional project management, than the process and customer engagement.

Each organization encounters distinctive challenges and usual problems that drive them to adopt agile. When you can define your problem, you have the starting point for agile. Now you can figure out how agile will address your issue and decide the KPI's, or Key Performance Indicators, founded on these motives. While agile may not be for every organization, there has yet to be any area discovered where it cannot be applied successfully. The best advice for adoption is to make sure the core values of agile align well with your philosophy as a business. It does not make sense to try to force the two to fit together.

Reasons for Adopting Agile

The best reason to adopt agile in your company is that of its proven success in a variety of fields and projects. The process is constantly changing and quickly evolving thanks to its flexible and self-improving qualities. Other reasons to adopt agile include: processes, self-regulation, accepting of change, fast turnaround, customer engagement, and motivated team environment.

Process for Excellence

The path to excellence lies in consistent actions no matter what business you run. This is why a business succeeds or fails; your actions are not individually spontaneous, they are practiced over and over. This means the processes you set up to complete your actions must be "right." Therefore, adopting an agile process can dramatically help your success because it focuses on continually improving your actions to deliver the highest value to your customers. In addition, it is abstract enough to allow for customization as required. Using the processes already in place in other companies or for other projects can be adapted to suit your company's needs. Then you can logically assess how it works for you.

Self-regulation

If you are not careful, when you establish an agile environment, the success can lead to a shift in priority. Your team members will move from task-focused to role-focused. Because of the process worked before, they do not want to stray from the structure of the company but rather stick with the flow. Without realizing it, it is possible you fall into a rigid bureaucracy. This type of environment removes the opportunity for taking risks, solving errors, or experimenting. This is why emphasizing the self-regulation inherent to successful agile processes is important. This focus encourages balancing flexibility and discipline. It is not bureaucratic; it is democratic. Having a strong, self-regulated agile process gives your team the opportunity to stay focused on the project and stay productive, instead of just completing steps to a process.

Accepting of Change

The creep that occurs in a project's scope or changes that are inherent to all tasks means it is important to accept and plan for change. The problem is that you cannot know what the changes will be until it is impossible to avoid it. Until that point, tasks are created to resist change. When it is impossible to escape, then procedures are implemented. This is not how an agile environment approaches change and creeping scope. Instead, change is at the forefront of the process. Change is an evolution, not a limitation. This means that as changes or issues come up, they should be responded to instead of avoided. Solutions do not come prepackaged, so your teams must try out a few options until one sticks.

Fast Turnaround

Projects can be vigorous and unpredictable. As a new concept hits the market, old ones are falling away just as fast. This means it cannot take a long time for you to develop something "perfect" before you get it to the customer. In a fast-paced world, a traditional project management approach can just simply take too long. Following the "old way" means you eventually have to choose between compromising on the customer's needs or your process. Becoming agile allows you to get a valuable product to market while still meeting the needs of the customer.

Customer Engagement

One of the major challenges in a traditional project management system is that you do not know if you met your customer's needs until you deliver the final project. This is because only the customer can tell you how they feel about the result. This separation creates an extreme problem. There have been a series of solutions proposed to handle this, but constant customer engagement throughout the process has been proven over and over again to be the best solution. This involves the customer in troubleshooting problems and addressing changes together with your teams, so they know the final solution they will receive. Creating this expectation at the beginning of the relationship allows you to emphasize the value you place on your customer more than a process.

Motivated Team Environment

Traditional project management spends a significant amount of time on planning and charting. While planning is still important, it is redirected to another place. Stakeholders used to determine roles that the project manager would assign to team members and then determine the timeline. The moment the plan was revealed to the team and the roles were assigned, it was strictly adhered to. Instead of it providing guidance and accountability to the project, it turned into a crutch that allowed the team to blame the failure or success of the project on the plan. This was because the accountability of the project was placed on the project manager, not on those carrying out the tasks. Using the agile method, the team can take ownership of the project. When the team felt that their effort was a direct benefit or hindrance to the overall project, they felt accountable and motivated to put their best work forward. The teams work together, not as individual "worker bees." Setting up an opportunity for teams to work together cross-functionally is another benefit to this, and makes individual teams rise to the challenge for others as well. If a team member is new, limited, or unskilled, they can still contribute to the project and group and feel important.

The final reason to adopt agile is simple; it makes you think smarter about your company, projects, customers, and employees. Chances are, if you have tried project management or are thinking about it, that is one of the best reasons to adopt agile immediately. But if that's not enough, consider the information outlined above: a new approach to your processes, self-regulation, accepting of change, fast turnaround, customer engagement, and motivated team environment. One or all should be enough to make you ready to try an agile approach on your next project.

Chapter 4: The 12 Principles and Four Values of Agile Project Management and the Agile Manifesto

It is amazing to try to comprehend the sheer volume of projects that have been completed thanks to the information released in the "Agile Manifesto." Prior to the release of this report, the process of project management was not necessarily a swift endeavor. Because of this lengthy process, countless projects that were scheduled to take place never happened because the company decided to go in another direction before they could even see the light of day. This resulted in companies lining up for a new process. They realized the flaws and were ready to try something new to address the current challenges of project management.

Part of the teachings from the manifesto included a definition of 12 principles and four values essential to an agile project. They were defined with a sole purpose: to change the way we approach a project, so it still delivers quality but in less time.

At the very core of any agile project is the "Agile Manifesto." While it is most often applied to software development, its application is beneficial anywhere. Its approach to communication, collaboration, and lean development is attractive to many industries. The overall plan broken into small tasks can be swiftly developed, making it another attractive feature for just about any company. Of course, as mentioned in the previous chapters, the adaptability to change is paramount to its success.

To better understand the foundation of the 12 principles and four values, it is important to establish a background on the "Agile Manifesto" and how it laid out the foundation for years to come. In addition, providing practical applications for some of the concepts explained is another important element. Both will be highlighted below to help you as you learn more about these 12 principles and four values.

The Agile Manifesto

In the 1990's, there was a general frustration that was occurring with traditional project management. There was a lapse of time between delivery and requirements. Customers ordered a specific application or feature on a task, but the solution often took longer than they could wait, so the projects were being canceled at an accelerated rate. This time lapse was affected by several factors: changes, the complexity of the primary requirements, and the company's process. When a project was completed, often the needs of the client or industry had changed, making the final product worthless. The traditional process failed to take advantage of the presence of constant change and the need for speed.

When a collaboration of minds gathered in 2001 to voice their frustrations together, they collectively came up with the "Agile Manifesto." These 17 leaders of industry met twice to talk about the topic: once in Oregon and the second time in 2001 in Utah. During this time, the 12 principles were also outlined. To quote the manifesto, "We are uncovering better ways of developing software by doing it and helping others do it. Through this work, we have come to value: individuals and interactions over processes and tools, working software over comprehensive documentation, customer collaboration over contract negotiation, responding to change over following a plan. That is, while there is value in the items on the right, we value the items on the left more."

The founding values mentioned above were vague enough to allow for adaptation and personal perception, but no matter what project is completed using an agile approach, it will apply each value in its own way, to lead the delivery and development of functional, prime products for your customers.

The Four Values

There are four distinct values outlined in the manifesto: "Through this work, we have come to value: individuals and interactions over processes and tools, working software over comprehensive documentation, customer collaboration over contract negotiation, responding to change over following a plan."

"Individuals and Interactions Over Processes and Tools"

This is the first value outlined in the manifesto. Intrinsically this implies it is quite possibly the most important value of the agile method according to the "Agile Manifesto." The leaders decided that the people involved in the project were more important than the tools or processes in place. The people are the ones responding to the needs of your company, and they drive the process. If it is the other way around like in the system that was traditionally used, the process drove the team. This hindered the team in their ability to react to changes and challenged them to meet the needs of the customer. For example, communication is different when the business values the process over the customer. If the company values individuals over processes, they are more likely to be flowing and constant. If there is a need for change, it is brought up and responded to immediately. If a company values the process over the individual, there is a schedule set for communication; each interaction comes with a clear expectation of what must be discussed.

"Working Software Over Comprehensive Documentation"

In a traditional project management approach, incredible amounts of time were dedicated to outlining the entire project from the beginning conceptualization to the final delivery. Tech specs, tech requirements, tech prospectus, design docs, test plans, doc plans, approvals, etc. were all required documentation. Completing all this documentation took time, which was time away from the actual project itself. This was often the reason for the project being delayed. The list of expected and comprehensive documentation was debilitating. While agile does not completely remove the need to document the process, it does offer a more streamlined approach. The goal is to give plenty of space to the teams to get the tasks completed, with the distraction of excess paperwork and little details removed. Typically, an agile document, for a software project specifically, is presented as a user story. This format is familiar to a developer and allows them to use the critical information to start creating a new response. While documentation is still a valuable part of the process, the functional software, or end project, is more valuable.

"Customer Collaboration Over Contract Negotiation"

When a company and a client sit down to discuss a project, negotiations occur where the 2 parties determine together how the project will be delivered, and the checkpoints necessary throughout the timeline where changes or additional details can be renegotiated. This is the traditional approach. The 2 parties would normally spend extreme amounts of time diving into all the details imaginable, typically before the project even began, to come up with a strategy. This meant the customer was involved in the beginning and end but not the middle when the work was actually taking place. To collaborate with the customer instead is completely the opposite. The manifesto discussed the ideal customer as one that is involved in the process and collaborates with the team for the duration of the project. The result of this approach showed the company's satisfaction with an easier delivery that the customer appreciated and knew met their needs. Sometimes the customer only engages during certain times for demonstrations or to touch base, but it is not uncommon to find a customer included daily with a team, being present in meetings, and checking in to make sure it will meet their needs in the end.

"Responding to Change Over Following A Plan"

Before, the change was a liability. It was an expense. It was planned for in the effort to avoid it. The plan to avoid it was to plan in detail how the project would proceed. This plan included a well-defined outline of deliverables with all actions typically considered as important as each other. In addition, the deliverables were often reliant on the delivery of other parts of the project being completed. It was like a large puzzle, where the next piece could not be placed until the previous one was laid down. Instead, with an agile approach, importance moves from one iteration to the next as needed, and change is expected to be part of the iteration and overall project. This means more value is added to the end result; it is not a liability.

The 12 Principles

You need to also know the 12 guiding principles introduced at the same time as the manifesto. These principles are what outline a successful company's environment where changes are encouraged and applauded, and the customer is the center of the process. In addition, the 12 principles also show the way to apply agile to the needs of your company.

Below is a description of the 12 principles of agile:

1. *"Customer satisfaction through early and continuous software delivery"*

    Instead of waiting a long time to get the product, a customer is more satisfied when they can see working products in stages more often in the process.

2. *"Accommodate changing requirements throughout the development process"*

    There will be changes required for the project. A requirement will change, or a new feature will be requested. It is important to be able to honor those changes without creating a delay in the delivery of the project.

3. *"Frequent delivery of working software"*

    Consistent and functioning products are feasible, thanks to the iterations lead by a Scrum master.

4. *"Collaboration between the business stakeholders and developers throughout the project"*

    Align your business team and your technical team. When they are working together, you will notice the improvement in the decisions being made.

5. *"Support, trust, and motivate the people involved"*

    If your team is unhappy, they are unmotivated. These teams do not produce good work. On the other hand, a team that is happy and motivated produces great work. Aim for the latter.

6. *"Enable face-to-face interactions"*

    Keep your team together. There is value to face-to-face communication during the iterations.

7. *"Working software is the primary measure of progress"*

    The best way to determine how you are doing on your project is to monitor the working products you can provide to your client throughout the project.

8. *"Agile processes to support a consistent development pace"*

    While the process is not the focus, it does become a habit. And with each completed agile project, the habit becomes more replicable and predictable. You can count on the average speed at which your team will operate consistently.

9. *"Attention to technical detail and design enhances agility"*

To withstand changes, enhance outputs, and keep up the speed of delivery, you need to make sure your teams have the necessary skill sets to produce quality work.

10. *"Simplicity"*

Make sure what you produce will meet the needs but not much more for the current moment.

11. *"Self-organizing teams encourage great architectures, requirements, and designs"*

Offering support to others on how to produce excellent products, engaging often with their teammates, owning their part in the process, and having the power to make decisions, are characteristics and actions of a motivated and skilled member of your team.

12. *"Regular reflections on how to become more effective"*

Provide the opportunity for team members to increase efficiency by supporting their self-improvement, process-improvement, skill advancement, and system advancement.

Chapter 5: The Three Premium Principles

The unfortunate side effect of the agile method is that there is no magic process or prescription to help you find a solution to your problem. While you cannot pick up an agile book and find a plan that you can plug and play, you can find tips on how to make your agile projects more successful. Below are the three of the premium principles you can implement to help your labors flourish.

1. *Make Your Loop for Feedback Short*

While many people identify the importance of an agile project, they struggle to define its importance. Simply put, the shorter time between working and getting customer input on the product is a founding purpose of it all. The nightmare of hiding away for extended periods of time to create an entire project only to show it to your customer who reacts negatively to the outcome can be entirely avoided with an agile approach. Daily or at least after each iteration, the customer is involved in the process and provides feedback. This feedback is included in the next iteration, as expected. In addition, a working product can be given to the customer after a sprint or cycle for development. This delivery gives your team the opportunity for immensely valuable reviews for future changes. When you incorporate the feedback into the next workable delivery, your customer can appreciate the value of the product and your company to them. Now you are no longer checking off boxes on a plan that was established before the challenges of the project were fully realized.

Another component that is usable in an agile project is to create a test for the task you are working on to determine its practical application in the overall project. This is called TDD, or Test-Driven Development, in a software agile environment. Coders write in a test for their piece of the project to test its overall usability before saying it is complete. If it passes the test, it is done. If not, the coder has the opportunity to find the problem and fix it before it affects other parts of the project. This process motivates team members to find the easiest and fastest method to the solution. There is no need to connect parts of the project or task unnecessarily. This concept encourages simplicity. In a coding environment, this simpler code also makes it easier for future changes and adaptations. While this feedback is not necessarily coming from the client, it is another method for shortening the cycle for feedback. While you may hear this concept referred to as another name, like Behavioral-Driven Development, or BDD, or Acceptance Test-Drive Development, or ATDD, there are differences between the approaches despite many similarities.

2. *Agile Works from the Inside*

Internally-focused products also need to be improved constantly. This means you also need to be aware of how you can keep your internal environment competitive to offer the best to your customers. You also need to be constantly improving. When you are offering a leading company that delivers value to customers, you will find intense competition for your open positions. Think of innovative companies, inside and out, like Microsoft, Netflix, Facebook, and Google. People compete to work with them because they do not only provide value to their customers, but a valuable place to work. In addition, these kinds of companies bring their development and operations teams together for the best results. Developers are making the products, doing sprints, and talking about Scrum. Operators are administrators and experts who manage and deploy the products. In a more traditional environment, development creates and then passes to the operations side to deploy. They would then manage the operations of the product to ensure it functions properly. The new challenge is to integrate the two together to become more agile.

To develop this integration, it is important to remove the barrier between the two departments. The two begin working together to get help on both designing and automating. This cross-functioning collaboration internally is vital to the success of an agile company. It helps each role receive important, internal feedback to perform better and provide more value. It is no longer a pass-off but rather a team sport.

3. *The value of the business is the focus*

Ideally, you have a goal that you are measuring your progress against, so you can have a shorter feedback loop. This means every iteration or sprint results in a workable product that operates simultaneously with other products. But the primary purpose does not rely on a singular function. The primary purpose is the value that is provided to the business, especially your customer's business. Your goal is to provide them a solution to deeply employ their customers or achieve more resourcefully.

A traditional project management process has a common problem: the conception of the end product is forced at the beginning, prior to any feedback or testing of an approach's success to a problem. During this process, the customer works with you to create a laundry list of needs, and then you develop what you think will respond to those needs. This type of process means you do not interact with the customer often, but the true challenge is the dependence on the list of needs set at the beginning rather than providing real value to the customer. Blaming the failure of the project on the list provided at the beginning is ineffective. A product will only work if it fulfills the current needs of the customer and ultimate user in the end.

Making your feedback cycle shorter, ensuring agile is working form the inside out, and focusing on the value of the business and product are the three primary principles of an agile project and company. They drive most of the successful businesses in your industry and set them above the more mediocre competition. If you focus on these three primary principles, you will almost surely improve your processes and company success.

Chapter 6: The Agile Litmus Test

It is hard not to jump on the agile-bandwagon. If you are not talking with trustworthy professionals about how to implement agile in your business, you can get a lot of sideline opinions about how it "should" be done or how it is "correctly" applied. While a litmus test will not guarantee your success, it can help you make sure you are ready to apply an agile approach. This chapter is dedicated to giving you some basic tips on how to apply agile to your projects.

Your Needs or Your Project's Needs

"Experts" are around every corner when you let people know you are thinking about agile. Some of them actually are experts, with developed skills over time and certifications, but others have the same initials behind their names with no practical experience. The problem is that, while both have the drive to help you, only one can be counted on. The other will probably be more harmful than helpful. To make sure you hire an expert and not a novice, consider this question: "How can I help them help me?" This question will make sure that you identify your needs before spending time and money working with a professional.

Another consideration is the process or method of agile you want to adopt. Just as there are countless "experts" out there, there are just as many ways you can adopt agile into your company. The perfect methodology fits with your company's needs, culture, and environment. This may mean the agile process is simple, but it can also mean it needs to be more pragmatic. To determine the best process, ask yourself: "How will I find an acceptable fit for my unique environment?" This question will make sure that you are considering your company's culture before making a decision about how you will adopt agile.

Another need you must consider is the need to measure the process and how it meshes with your team, leadership, and overall organization. A measurement can be based on numbers, observations, or it can be situational. For example, you could set an ideal number of agile projects you expect your teams to hit and wait to see if they are completing agile projects at the rate you expected. You can also observe your team's interactions to determine if their approaches are more agile than traditional. Watch how people interact with one another or speak about a task they are working on to observe if they are approaching it in line with the principles and values of an agile environment. A situational measurement looks at a process, project, or procedure and compares it with real-world challenges. Because the focus of agile is on producing functional products over processes, it is important that the scenario falls in line with a more realistic expectation rather than ideal. Whatever measurements you determine, you need to ask yourself if they are appropriate for the outcomes or for simply making you feel good about your work. Do they indicate the health of the project, or your pride? This question you can ask yourself will help you determine this answer: "How do I make sure that my measurements in place offer value and insight to produce results that I can take action on, so my teams can make decisions based on data?"

Your Focus and Simplicity

With all the vague or complex options available, how can you ensure that you know how to incorporate agile into your efforts and be successful? Thankfully, one of the main principles of agile is its the simplicity. You need to be focused on keeping it that way to make sure you stay simple, so you keep the outcome at the forefront. A simple method for incorporating agile into your company is to begin with the foundational concepts and then compare them to the important aspects of your company: the needs of your business, employees, and customers. With this perspective, you can adjust your agile approach while continuing to measure your results to improve your outcomes. Below is a short litmus test you can perform to make sure you are always focused and simple:

1. *Are you in line with the "Agile Manifesto?"*

   In order to fully understand what agile is and how to start with the foundational concepts at your company level, you should read the manifesto. From there, learn the 12 principles and four values. Thankfully you already know what they are thanks to the previous chapter, but if you are still hazy about what one of them means or how it functions in your environment, you need to learn more about it. Consider breaking apart the principles into a set of value-laden words that you are clear on and can use to shape your decisions. Make sure the words you choose from the principle align with the intentions of the authors. As you begin to introduce this to your company, it may be worth your time to have all your employees or leaders do this exercise as well.

2. *What are you going to use to measure your agile performance?*

   While there is a chapter in this book that identifies three of the primary principles in an agile environment, these may not be the most significant to you or your customers. If this is the case, look at each of the principles and choose three that are best for your company. They should not be chosen from your singular perspective. Gathering your teams, host a workshop, and get the important people to honestly choose the top three from their perspectives.

Completing this is a test in itself. If you host several workshops with your employees but get a variety of answers, not aligned with or close to one another, you need to stop the process and address this cultural problem first. All your key people must be on the same page before proceeding. The danger you face without focusing on this alignment is that important players will not feel included and will work against each other instead of toward the uniform outcome. Sometimes finding this homeostasis is a challenge, so make sure you spend time working it out fully before rushing ahead.

After you align your team and determine the three primary principles for your organization, you will use these to indicate the measurement of your litmus test. They become your KIs, or Key Indicators. In addition, these three principles are now your outcomes you strive for during an agile project. If a project meets these three principles, than you can feel certain it performed the way you intended.

3. *How can you execute a critical assessment?*

Using the KIs you identified in the previous step, you now need to determine how far or close you are to each question. A standard litmus test uses a scale from 1 to 14. Try a scale from 1 to 7 instead. This provides an odd range to help make sure you get a more synthesized response. A "1" indicates you are far from your target, while "7" indicates that you have met the objective. You should not be the only one evaluating the project. Make sure to include other members equally and stress that responses should be fair. Each respondent should share their perspective in an unbiased manner. While not all team members can participate sometimes, representatives from each group should be included as much as is realistic.

Hosting facilitated sessions is often beneficial during this process. You need to have honest and open communication. The intention behind the questions and answers should be transparent. Some members may not feel safe to open up in a large or medium-sized group, or in general. Account for this by offering an opportunity for anonymous responses, like writing reviews that do not offer a place to write their names, or anonymous evaluation forms. Offering a one-on-one session may be beneficial, but it is often ineffective in a larger setting.

4. *What actions will I encourage to align with our agile approach?*

After you have reviewed the responses related to your KIs, it is important to decide what actions you will take to address anything lower than 6. Determining the actionable items allows you to host a planning session with key players to decide what strategies you will employ to get you nearer to attaining your desired goals. It is also important to look for responses to certain KI questions that are wide-ranging. This shows that team members are not aligned, and it is a gap that should be addressed.

During the follow-up meetings, ask questions like, "What needs to happen to get us closer to a 6 or 7 on this topic?" and, "What can our stakeholders and customers be doing to help us get closer to this expectation?" Other questions should focus on the approach taken that got you to where you were and ask, "What can be changed or improved to help us become more agile?"

Keep in mind that the questions and answers are meant to determine meaningful actions, not prideful measures. This may mean also asking for feedback on the questions themselves that resulted in the number arrived at. Ask your team, "How can the measures or metrics be more meaningful and accurately provide actionable responses to help us become more agile?"

When the groups define at least one action to implement as a result of the conversations, it is now your role to make sure the actions are implemented, and each person is held accountable. After the next project, measure the actions to see if the performances move closer to the goal and continue the conversation until a solution, or a score of 6 or 7, is found.

5. *Are you continuing to grow and reassess over time?*

As you move forward with the agile process, you need to remember needs and goals change constantly. This means your process needs to change as well. Keep revisiting the primary principles and processes in place to make sure you are offering the best outcomes.

Now that you can give your process a litmus test which is customized to your company, here are some basic questions you can ask to get your measurement process started:

1. Will the desired, valuable outcome realistically materialize with our current actions? Are we completing actions continuously to deliver this goal?

2. Is change welcome and used in our process?

3. Is there daily collaboration between the customer and our team? If it is not daily, is close engagement occurring often?

4. Is the outcome obtainable with the support provided to the teams?

5. Is there face-to-face communication occurring more frequently than email and phone conversations?

6. Is the working product the measurement for progress?

7. Is the current work pace sustainable for the long-term?

8. Are the choices and work being produced valuable and also adaptable to chance?

9. Are the actions being taken, simple and focused? For example, are teams making decisions and taking action to get solutions with as little "extra" as possible?

10. Are you supported to be successful within your own self-managed system? Do you have the autonomy to organize your members as the task requires?

11. Is there adequate opportunity to review and amend your behaviors and actions as needed?

You can use the above-mentioned scoring system of 1 to 7 to determine how you are doing with your current agile process, or you can have members simply answer "yes" or "no." If all the questions are answered "yes," you can feel confident your agile system is functioning in place. Any questions that receive a "no" require review. This means that they need to be questioned and teams need to provide suggestions on how the answer can be moved to a "yes." Continuous review of the process and success of your agile environment means continuous valuable work being produced internally and externally for your customers, making you an indispensable player in your industry.

Chapter 7: Agile Methodologies - Lean, Scrum, XP, Kanban, Crystal, FDD

Practices, characteristics, and philosophies are very similar no matter what method of agile you choose to implement. The differences are only highlighted when you go to implement it. The way practices are applied, the terms used or tactics employed, varies from method to method. Throughout this chapter, you will learn about some of the more popular methodologies including: Scrum, Lean, Kanban, Crystal Methodology, and Feature-Driven Development (FDD).

Scrum

Possibly the most popular method is the Scrum method. It is a simple framework that can be applied to a broad spectrum of projects. You can control and manage iterations and project increments of all sizes. Even in the last ten years, Scrum has evolved to be more and more applicable in an agile environment. The reasons people flock to Scrum is because it is simple, productive, and actionable.

The method works by having a "product owner" collaborating with teams to find and rank projects into a list called the "product backlog." This log contains features requested, fixes proposed for bugs, requirements that do not function, and more. When you find something that needs to be completed, you can provide a functional product you need and add it to the log. The owner drives the priorities and teams made of inter-department members agreeing to provide deliverable parts of the product during a sprint. These sprints are usually given 30 days to complete the task. When the owner defines the log and commits it to the sprint, no additional items can be added to it. Only the team can override the log's commitment to additional tasks. After the sprint is done and delivered, the log is revisited and re-ranked. After analyzing the backlog, the next steps are chosen for the next sprint.

When you decide to adopt the Scrum method after following a more traditional project management form, you can expect it to be one of the easiest transitions. You can still plan in advance like before, but the timeline is faster as well as the communication and feedback being more frequent. Those that do well in a Scrum environment include businesses and customers who want to work closely together to produce and see working samples and offer feedback for the next iteration.

Lean

Based on the Lean Enterprise Movement, the Lean agile method concentrates on providing valuable products to the customer and an efficient "value stream." The value stream includes the way you plan to deliver the value.

The primary principles for a lean project are:

- Remove unnecessary surplus
- Intensify learning
- Make decisions when absolutely necessary
- Provide valuable deliverables before it is absolutely necessary
- Inspire the team
- Shape reliability
- Visualize the complete picture

Removing unnecessary surplus occurs by prioritizing the most value-loaded tasks for a project and producing them one at a time. This allows you to stress an efficient and speedy work process and gives back feedback swiftly and reliably. Small teams and individual team members make decisions which gives them the authority to have control of their process. It also allows each team member to be useful and productive in their own way.

Kanban

Similar to Scrum, Kanban helps your teams work closely with each other. It stresses continuous production without placing all the expectations on the development side.

There are 3 primary principles in a Kanban agile method:

1. Picture your workflow for the day. Imagine how each component will work with the others.
2. Minimize the amount of "WIP" or "Work in Progress." By keeping the workload light at any given time, the team can balance their efforts without feeling overcommitted.
3. Improve the flow. Make sure the highest-priority item is accomplished and then move to the next one on the backlog.

This implementation method provides a continual learning process, strong collaboration, and defined team workflows.

XP or Extreme Programming

While this methodology is popular, it does not come without its controversy. Unlike the other methods described above, this implementation method is more rigid. Aligned with the agile manifesto, XP focuses on involving the customer in the process, short feedback loops, frequent measurement, ongoing development, and team collaboration so that functional work is provided frequently, ideally no longer than three weeks.

The four values of XP include: courage, feedback, communication, and simplicity.

The 12 practices of XP include:

1. Development game
2. Little deliverables
3. Tests for customer agreement
4. Simplicity in design
5. Coupled coding
6. Tested deliverables
7. Refactoring
8. Continual incorporation
9. Shared possession
10. Standards for development
11. Allegory
12. Maintainable speed

"User stories" are developed alongside the customer based on their collaborative definition of priority deliverables. As each iteration is completed, your teams need to deliver functionality according to the high-priority "user stories" after they've estimated and planned the process for that unit. There is a framework in place that is simple and supportive of the process, so your productivity is maximized.

Crystal

This process is the most simple and easy to adopt than all the other methodologies introduced thus far. Under the umbrella of Crystal, there exists a host of other options such as "Crystal Clear," "Crystal Yellow," "Crystal Orange," etc. Each demi-method implements specific elements customized by the size of your team, the importance of the project, and priorities established. This approach is in response to the need for custom tailoring of practices, policies, and processes for the unique project needs. Several of the priority principles of Crystal include: simplicity, communication, teamwork, and frequent reviews for improved processes. Crystal aligns with the agile manifesto because of its alignment with key topics like involving the customer often, a focus on change and adaptation, simplifying the bureaucratic process, and providing early and frequent working deliverables.

DSDM or Dynamic Systems Development Method

In the 1990s, an alternative solution to the challenges in the software industry was proposed called RAD or Rapid Application Development. This was more effective than what was being used; however, it did not evolve effectively for the demands of the industry. This then led to the creation of DSDM in 1994. The goal was to institute a standard for the industry, so it was more of a uniform framework for rapidly delivering a project. Since 1994, DSDM has grown to offer a more all-inclusive ground level for companies to scale, execute, manage, and plan their agile approach and projects.

There are nine principles that ground the DSDM methodology. Each principle is centered around the needs and values of the business, consistent customer engagement, motivated team members, rapid and continual deliveries, testing built into the process, and users involved in the process. Within the DSDM method, implementers adhere to the philosophy that 80% of a functional deliverable is implemented in 20% of the time invested.

DSDM also has a set of rules practitioners follow nicknamed "Moscow." The acronym stands for:

M- *"Must have requirements"*

S- *"Should have, if possible"*

C- *"Could contain, but not necessary"*

W- *"Will not be included now, but could be added later"*

The important work is a must for successful completion, but not all work assigned falls into this category. Most of the time, the critical components are included in the iteration expectations with 'should haves' or 'could contains,' so if there is a time they could be included—or if not—they can be let out without sacrificing the high-priority items to stay on schedule. It is possible to run this method alongside other methodologies, or on its own.

FDD or Feature-Driven Development

This methodology is the result of several leadership minds: Stephen Palmer, Jon Kern, Paul Szego, Lim Bak Wee, M.A. Rajashima, and Jeff De Luca. FDD. It was originated during a collaborative effort between Jeff De Luca and Peter Coad, the OOD "Thought Leader." They contrived a process that had increasingly shorter iterations and was driven by models. To begin, the project creates a general shape to the model. After, the teams take two weeks to complete their iterations. These short sprints are to design and build a deliverable. Each feature is little, but usable for the customer. After these iterations, the remainder of the project is approached with the intention of delivering features by utilizing the primary eight processes:

1. "Domain Object Modeling"
2. "Developing by Feature"
3. "Component/Class Ownership"
4. "Feature Teams"
5. "Inspections"
6. "Configuration Management"
7. "Regular Builds"
8. "Visibility of progress and results"

Practices such as "Component or Class Ownership" and "Regular Builds" are specific recommendations for developers using the FDD methodology. Those that successfully use the FDD method, state that it is easier and more scalable than many other options and is best for large teams working on large projects. What is unique about FDD from other methods is that it identifies precise and timely work sprints that are independent of the overall project. In a software environment, this includes *Promote to Build, Code Inspection, Code, Design Inspection, Design,* and *Domain Walkthrough.*

Chapter 8: How to Establish Agile Roles

Creating a thriving team is one of the most important indicators for success when you migrate to an agile environment. As a matter of fact, the agile migration will not be successful without collaborative teams that work together efficiently and effectively together. In order to establish your agile roles, you need to do more than just define them and plug in your team members. Instead, you must develop each role with the clear intention of project finality, not just the preparation for the project.

This means you need to change your mindset. No longer are you ruled by the questions, "What is needed to complete the project and who do I have who can work on it?" These two questions can fill a defined role, but the people you have "available" may not be the best for the team or project's needs. Instead, you need to build a team that is diverse and balanced. The members should be both in possession of the skill to accomplish the tasks but also the interpersonal strengths to get it done as a collaborative team. They need to be dependable, flexible, willing, and creative. The combination of technical skill and these personality traits makes for a dynamic and successful team. And the final component of a successful team is the support you provide to them and the support they provide to one another. This goes beyond simply training them how to *be* agile, but encouraging and supporting them as they adjust to the process is paramount.

Approaching the assignment of roles also depends on the size of the team you are working with. For example, a large environment offers more people to choose from, but more complications from previous roles. A small environment offers a speedier alteration to roles, but less to pull from. To help you define roles for your organization, the following chapter has been separated into small and large teams. Small is considered a team with fewer than 15 people and large is a team with more than 50. Teams that fall in between these numbers should read about both suggestions and come up with a solution they think will work best for their unique situation.

Small Teams

Each methodology names their roles slightly differently; however, many of the descriptions will align with the roles listed below. At times, you will find alternative titles listed in the description to help you find the best role for your method. It is important to remember that a role is not a position in your company. A person can have multiple roles, and those roles can change occasionally or frequently depending on your company and the projects. In addition, it is possible to have more than one person assigned to a role, or no one at all. Below are the most common small-team agile roles:

Team Leader

Also known as "Scrum Master," "Team Coach," or "Project Lead." The person in this role oversees the teams and gathers the resources necessary for the team's success. They also protect the team from outside threats. This role is more administrative, requiring more inter-personal management skills rather than technical. It is considered better to leave these technical components to the teams to work on, anyway.

Team Members

Also known as "Developer" or "Programmer." These people create and deliver the project pieces. During this process, these people model, program, test, and deliver features.

Product Owner

Also known as "On-site Customer," "Active Stakeholder," or "Stakeholder." This role is reserved for a single person dedicated on the team to review the backlog and determine the priorities. They are responsible for making sure that decisions are speedy and also offer information quickly.

Stakeholder

Also known as "Direct User," "Indirect User," "User Manager," "Senior Manager," "Operations Manager," etc. This role is assigned to the person who is paying for the completion of the project, supports the team administratively, audits the work, or generally manages the personnel. Anyone affected by the project are considered stakeholders in the project and should be included as such.

Technical Experts

These people are responsible for stepping in to help a team complete a task, but are not a consistent member of the task force. For example, a build master may need to be called upon to write a script or a DBA needs to be used to design and test a system. They provide a certain skill set when needed or help with a problem, and then they back out of the iteration.

Domain Experts

These people are also temporary members of the team that collaborate with the members. The people who are assigned this role are experts in a certain area, such as an expert in taxes who comes in to teach about the requirements needs from a legal perspective or an executive from a sponsor who shares the project's vision with the team.

Independent Tester

This is more than one person, generally. This group of people is not involved in the day-to-day production of the feature, but rather come in when the product is ready to be tested. They can work alongside the team, but their intention is to validate the work of the team. Many companies utilize this role when they have adequate staffing, but it is not required for your success. If you find yourself unable to keep an independent test team all the time, consider only assigning this role for the more detailed or large-scale projects.

Large Teams

After totalling over 20 people in a team, it is time to reconsider your roles assigned. Technically, a team is not "large" until it is over 50, but the dynamic shift between 19 and 20 is significant enough to warrant a new look. Now you may have enough to divide up and conquer more even faster! Now you can have two small teams instead of one of larger size. Ideally, these small teams can work independently to complete the agile task, often part of a larger project. This idea is often referred to as "Conway's Law" in reference to Melvin Conway, the man who outlined this concept toward the end of the 1960s. New roles for larger teams include:

Architecture Owner

This role facilitates the decisions of the architecture for the smaller teams and works closely with the overall architect owner, who manages the total direction of the architecture for the project. They lead the team to envision the architecture, because they helped develop the total vision in the beginning. This role should not be confused with the traditional architect because they are not creating the direction of the entire project, but rather, assisting with the formation and development of the plan.

Integrator

When there are two or more sub-teams or small teams working for a larger project, at some point the sub-teams need to integrate their work. At times, there will be a large team working on a complicated task, while there are a few small teams working on smaller iterations. Integrators gather the pieces from the various teams and begin to build them together into the final project. This role functions well with independent testers it has been assigned, because as the integrator combines the pieces, it is important to test the combination to make sure it functions properly.

The Absence of Traditional Roles

It may sound like most of the "old" roles have been eliminated, but after careful consideration, it is evident that these "new" agile roles combine what used to be the Project Manager or Business Analyst, with roles like Team Coach or Team Members. This means the functions of those roles still occur, but in a different capacity than before.

The Absence of Enterprise Roles

The primary purpose of this chapter has been to identify the team and organizational roles on an agile team, not on the role of an enterprise-level support, like the Enterprise Admin or Portfolio Manager. To be able to scale your agile methods better, you need to also create enterprise-level agile positions. While they may not hold a role on the teams, they can and should still embrace the agile mindset for the betterment and success of the teams and company in general.

Chapter 9: How to Create an Agile Environment

You cannot just change your processes to become an agile environment. The changes must occur at your company's cultural level. This is often the most challenging part. This is a challenge for a host of reasons, such as comfort or fear of change, but once addressed, you can begin to create the agile environment you are looking for. You should address your culture head on, and show how you and all the management above the team members plan to support them as they adopt the agile mindset.

For Small Companies

Because you lack the complex and high-tiered levels of larger corporations, it will be easier for you to adopt an agile environment. To create this culture, it is important to embrace and practice three principles: team members know what and how agile will be implemented into the company, mid-level managers stop directing and begin coaching, and executives validate the principles of an agile environment.

A Manager for Agile Methodology

An agile manager does not have a technical function. They simply operate as an inter-personal shepherd. They do not wield power to command their employees but rather develop respect over time. They communicate effectively, think analytically with the team, use diplomacy, and listen to understand and enhance a relationship.

To be a successful agile project manager, you need to realize that you are not the "boss" of the team members. You have no authority over them, so in order for you to get their involvement, you need to get the buy-in from their superiors before requesting them to be a part of the team. Before they can buy in to assign their employee to a team, the mid-level managers need to be trained in agile and express their support for this migration. It is ineffective to get buy-in from an employee before getting their manager's buy-in. For example, the manager needs to support the 10-minute stand up for the team's expectations for the day and project updates, which occurs daily. After the initial training, the best way to get buy in from all levels is to show you how they can be applied every day in your own role. You are the example that they look to when they need guidance.

Plan for "Just Enough"

This means you are only planning for what you need to deliver, and nothing more. You offer "just enough" to make sure you are on the right track before adding in more. It is a hard habit to create but essential to your success as an agile company. This shift in mentality, however, allows you to be able to deliver something tangible often.

As each iteration is provided to the customer, you get feedback to ensure the end result is valuable to the client. To make sure the customer is satisfied with the project, follow the 3 stages below:

1. Define the customer clearly. It is important that you and your team know exactly who your customer is and what they are specifically needing.

2. Create a strong relationship with the customer. You need to know your customer well. As a manager, it is ideal to communicate and engage your customer before the project even begins, so they want to talk to you throughout the process.

3. Advocate for the customer throughout the project. If the customer is not in the room while tasks are being discussed and prioritized, think like the customer and act in their best interest.

For Those Who Do Not Have a Technical Background

As discussed earlier, a manager does not need to have the technical skill to do their job, but it is important that they understand the expectations of the client and the team's ability to deliver. If you do not have a technical background, consider the following:

- Encourage your teams to test functionality often and in small doses, so you know it works before being added to the larger project. This allows you to find errors with your team before it becomes a large problem.

- Encourage automatic testing to make it easier on your teams.

- Conduct a daily test to give another opportunity to find errors early.

- Keep scale in mind so the process can grow organically.

The focus is on the team environment and not on how the code or project is developed. Make sure you communicate face-to-face more often than not, and model the behavior you want to see in the teams. Part of this means you cannot be more prideful than agile. Criticism of your concepts does not mean it is a personal attack, and the agile environment you are trying to create will crumble if you think like this. Stay positive and constructive, even if upset, and remember respect for others above all else.

How to Lead a Self-Owned Team

It is important that you guide your team from buy-in to ownership. As you begin adopting agile in your company, the team will begin buying in to the process. To morph from buy-in to ownership, the team needs to believe in the success of the process and consider it an ordinary procedure. At this point, a manager does not need to prod them to use the agile methods; they *want* to.

Not everyone will own the process at the same time, and that can occur because of his or her maturity and competency. Thankfully, through the agile process, these hindrances can be eradicated naturally. Part of the process is rewarding the effort put into an agile process. Much of this reward should be based on the team members' ability and willingness to collaborate.

It is also important to recognize the stage a team member is in with their career. New employees are learning and adapting already and rely on others to help them integrate into the new culture. Those who are contributing individually are the majority of your team and have a range of abilities. They are the ones who need to be managed and mentored. These people have already found their "comfort zone," so will take more time changing to a new method. The coaches on your team are those who love mentoring others and sharing their knowledge. If you get these people on board, they can help motivate the individuals to move from resenting the change to adopting it more easily.

Get Ownership from the Executives

Your executive team will ask some pointed and important questions, such as: why pursue an agile method, what is its value to the company, how much will this implementation cost, what are the inherent risks, and what will it do for the executives?

Being well-researched and confident in your approach to agile will help you in this conversation as well as finding answers to these common questions. Some of the answers will differ from company to company and project to project, so make sure you are upfront about what you are presenting and realistic in your expectations. It is also wise to make sure frequent communication occurs at the executive level, so they are in the loop and on board at all times.

Chapter 10: Agile Sprint Planning, Execution, and Reviewing

A sprint always contains certain elements that include how collaboration between team members should occur so incremental production of quality products can occur. It all begins on the first day of planning. This is not your typical project management planning; it is sprint planning. This requires the entire team to gather and plan the sprint together. This step is crucial to the process of planning. But before the team assembles, there is a preplan that should occur. You need to establish the backlog, so there are enough details and criteria. Then, the Product Owner needs to order the backlog and prepare to discuss the goals for the sprint with the team. Ideally, the goals desired should be mirrored in the prioritization of the backlog. And finally, you should estimate the workload of the desired teams. If you have done sprints with the teams before, you will be able to determine this more accurately. However, early adoption estimations may be inaccurate and require more discussion with the team to find a good balance.

Planning

During this planning phase, you and the team must determine the order of work to be completed by prioritizing the most valuable at the top. This way, as each sprint is completed, you can be confident you are providing working products that are the most important. It is a collaborative process. During this collaboration, you must settle on a "Sprint Goal." This goal identifies and defines the purpose of the work chosen. It defines the process of collaboration and revision as necessary.

This goal naturally leads to the plan of work. Now that you know what is most important to your end project and what you plan to accomplish first you can start coming up with how you will get to the end. This can be a technical plan or an estimate for the work required to be completed for the sprint. This planning process does not require the Product Owner in person, and in most cases, it is best if they are not in the room during this stage to encourage self-ownership, but they should be accessible if questions arise or clarification if needed. When the team is done planning, they should all feel confident in the forecast for the sprint to meet the Sprint Goal. Then they can *be* the execution of the plan while tracking the progress according to the outlined plan.

Execution

Every day the team will work on their tasks. They will need to work together and track how they are completing their tasks. During this execution, the team can show their progress on a board designated for their tasks and check in on the Spring Burndown to identify what work still remains to be accomplished. The consistent update by each team member is essential to the success and reliance of the rest of the team.

Another part of the execution includes daily 10 to 15-minute Scrum meetings. These should happen each day at the same time, in the same place. This is a place to plan how the team needs to move forward toward the goal. The people at the Scrum meeting should only be team members and each person should engage in the meeting. Participation comes in the form of explaining what was done the previous day to reach the goal, what they plan to do that day to reach the goal, and what challenges they are facing to reach the goal. After the Scrum meeting is done, the day should be clearly outlined regarding how the team will move toward the goal and what collaboration is required to accomplish it. The challenges facing the team should also be addressed by the Scrum Leader and Project Owner.

Another part of the Scrum process includes revisiting the backlog on a consistent basis. This does not happen at a certain time or place, but as details or changes occur, the backlog should be revisited. Each team will decide how often and when to review the backlog, but it can be a good practice to do every day. Whatever you settle on with your team, make sure the refinement process does not take more than 10% of your time during the sprint. If this means you cannot do it every day, you need to do it often, so the project stays on schedule.

When the backlog is presented to the team, the group must identify each element and review the scope and criteria required for completion. Then the team will break down large items if necessary and refine as needed. A timer is set to make sure the team does not spend too much time on the refinement process. When the timer is done, the team pauses and reconvenes later during the next planned refinement session. This keeps going and going, starting over when the last aspect is refined until the project is completed.

This collaboration is not isolated to the Scrum meetings and refinement sessions. It is consistent. The team owns all the success and failure of the product. Team members provide feedback, ask for and give help, and find work that needs to be done when their contribution is complete.

Reviewing

If the Sprint Goal is met, it is most likely because the team collaborated together and worked through risks and challenges. The team members have worked on the burndown to make sure the work was completed on time and involved the stakeholders in the process. This final step in the process should be a positive and motivational event, even if the result was less than expected. But it does not mean there should be no preparation going into the meeting. This review period provides the team the opportunity show off their work and how it contributes value to the overall project. These are also good opportunities to bring in the stakeholders to see the results. Make sure to invite them prior to the meeting time so they can plan on attending.

Reviewing your sprint also includes the opportunity to inspect your work and adapt it for future sprints. Performance reviews can be shared, feedback can be given, and lessons can be learned regarding the backlog prioritization. If work still remains to be completed, it can be reviewed and added back to the backlog as needed.

Retrospective

The review process looks at the product and deliverables' value to the project. It discusses the work that was done and identifies what was not done. When this is over, the retrospective can begin. This looks into the process the team followed to complete the sprint. It seeks to find the most efficient process. Hold this meeting as soon as possible prior to the review. This is optimal, because the review shines a light on ideas to be discussed during the retrospective.

Anyone can attend the retrospective, and the more participation, the better. The reason you want to encourage a variety of attendees is that each person involved in the sprint can own the process. This session must be honest and clear to allow people to air their feelings and observations with the aim for resolutions. Everyone who attends this session is equal to one another. The Scrum Master leads the meeting and prompts the discussion along the lines of how the process function did well this time, how did it break down, what participants think will make it better, and praise for exceptional performance from individual members. Another point of this meeting is to give a visual timeline of the sprint to help those in attendance remember certain actions throughout the process.

Chapter 11: Agile Quality Management

In an agile project, ensuring quality means that the processes to deliver a valuable product and project are well managed. The customer's satisfaction with the value-laden product is the ultimate measurement for the quality of product being delivered. Because this is inherently part of the agile process, you can assume then that quality management is also a natural part of the process. You can more specifically tackle the quality management through the following:

- The life cycle of an agile project

- The roles assigned to an agile project

- The initiation and scope of the agile project

- The planning and estimation of the agile project

- The execution, monitoring, and control of the agile project

- The total quality management of the agile project

- The risk management of an agile project

- The change management of an agile project

- The closure of an agile project

Quality Assurance and Control for An Agile Project

"Assurance" refers to the planned activities, while "control" refers to the implementation of the plans. In a traditional project management system, quality assurance and control occurred when the project manager created a detailed plan for the project. In an agile project, the two are already included in the process. This is because the expectation is that the agile team meets the needs defined recently by the customer, not what was written by the project manager, sometimes months previous to the current sprint. The product owner is a part of the daily team progress, so they can guide the process continually. While they are not involved completely, they can be present and check in to make sure everything is moving toward a valuable product for the customer.

Another built-in factor includes the Timebox. This concept means that there is a final time set for a deliverable. During the time specified, the team must create a functioning and valuable product for the customer according to the prioritized backlog. Frequent informal reviews and documented brainstorming sessions are helpful with this process. If there is a meeting, make sure someone is assigned the role of note-taker, so they can record the main topics reviewed and can send them to the team after the meeting as a refresher. These can also be sent to the Product Owner or other relevant stakeholders.

After a Timebox is completed there is a review meeting for the event. Of course, you can have more reviews during the Timebox, or longer Timeboxes such as those up to four weeks long. The documentation of the process is possibly one of the most important aspects of the process. Some methodologies "require" documentation while others simply recommend it. Whatever the case, it is a good practice to establish as long as it does not take too long to accomplish.

Additional assurances and controls built into the agile process include:

- Status meetings being held frequently

- Unit tests that are automated

- Acceptance tests

- Tried improvement

- Regression tests

- Exploratory tests

- Specialist tests

- Code review and metrics

- Constant incorporation

- Enlightening space

- Project reviews scheduled formally

Daily meetings satisfy the frequent meeting expectation. Products are tested as they are developed to make sure they perform 100% of the time, as they were intended to perform. Sometimes, the test can be developed even before the product! Other tests, such as the acceptance, regression, and exploratory test, require a definition of the issue and the creation of a plan to address the concern. In an acceptance test, it should be another automated process that makes sure the customer is still on board with the direction of the project and iteration. As more sprints are completed and pieces are added from other teams, it is important to test for regression. With the additions or changes, did the result not meet expectation? Again, this should be an automated process.

Another test, the exploratory test, is an unscripted test to show new challenges that have arisen. Some can and need to be addressed immediately while others can be added to the backlog to handle later. Specialist testing refers to additional testing that focuses on the outcome of a particular item, not the whole sprint or project at large. Test-driven development is a test-like measurement. It is another automated test and shows if the product passes or fails the technical and customer needs.

Code review and metrics allows testers to know what to test for. It can be done through traditional methods like walking through a code or by pair programming. A standard agile environment does create or hold on to information about the success of a project, but it can be a hard part to let go these days. The purpose of the metrics is to ensure each task is valuable and of the highest quality during the length of the project. Part of this process includes a regression test automated during each check-in. Sometimes this occurs multiple times a day.

The workspace provided for your teams should be motivational and informative. Key visuals should be in the room: Timebox plans, Burndown charts, Current Build Status, and more. This gives you the opportunity to check on the quality of the situation. The final review exists to show off the overall completed project. This gives the team time to celebrate and brainstorm how to be even better the next time.

Quality Improvement

Reviews and retrospectives are used to reflect on an agile project. The time spent in these meetings is designed to give honest accounts of how the process and time frame worked and how it can be improved next time. If there is a large change that comes out of these meetings, it is turned into a "User Story" for future implementation. Most of the time this is turned into a new sprint. Otherwise, the smaller changes can be added to the next sprint for speedy adaptation.

These improvements are based on one of the founding principles of agile: "At regular intervals, the team reflects on how to become more effective, then tunes and adjusts its behavior accordingly."

Coming from a traditional project management environment, quality control and improvement can be an additionally cumbersome process, detracting from your already utilized time. With an agile approach, you are checking and monitoring frequently through the process and again at the end. This checks-and-balances approach means you do not need to go far out of your way to make sure what you deliver is in line with the expectations of the client and your company.

Chapter 12: Agile Risk Management

Similar to the discussion in the previous chapter on quality management, risk management is an inherent part of the agile process. There are multiple factors that impact the success of a project, which is not part of the agile process, but when these are the only factors to be considered, the risk is significantly minimized already. Including a management plan for some of these risks can only aid your agile process. There are six steps in the circle of risk management in an agile process. The steps are:

1. ID
2. Categorize
3. Measure
4. Design
5. Undertake plan
6. Repeat

The Foundational Concepts

A risk means your project could fail, despite skillful team members and an agile plan. This is because a risk influences the project and results from uncertainty. Analyzing the risk allows the team to remove the uncertainty in the risk to minimize the effect it can have on the outcome of the project. Risk Mitigation or Risk Management is a plan the team develops together to anticipate, enclose or alleviate the effects of the risk.

While change is anticipated in an agile environment, risk is not the same thing. This is why you need to understand and accept that no matter the size of your company or the project, you will face a certain amount of risk. Planning a response to potential risks means you can minimalize the effect of the risk when it befalls you.

The Steps of Agile Risk Management

1. *ID*

    There are dimensions in risk. Some can be helpful or harmful, or a mixture of the two. The other dimensions of risk include internal influence or external impact. You can turn the dimensions of the risk into a SWOT analysis, or identify the Strengths, Weaknesses, Opportunities, and Threats of the risk. Risk management looks mainly at the analysis derived from the dimension of harm.

2. *Categorize*

Now the risks, after they have been identified, need to be categorized. This categorization occurs according to the area of the project the risk could affect, the reality of the risk occurring, and the total impact it could wield on the end result. Things like scope or resources primarily interest and impact the development team members, while other areas effect everyone, like the budget or security.

3. *Measure*

When you identify and categorize the risk, you are now ready to measure it. The best method to measure the risk is to assess it with two vectors: impact and probability. At this point, a professional needs to step in, especially if security is involved. The Project Owner is not a technical member, so they are most likely not an expert in the area in which the risk has been categorized. This is why you need to find someone who knows to come in and be objective with the measurement. At times you will find this person already in the team setting; other times you will need to look around the office or hire someone. This separation of the Project Owner from the measurement also takes off real or perceived pressure to produce something to make the team look good, despite a looming risk. After the matrix is released, meet with your team to discuss where things fall regarding these two points, and collaborate to find potential solutions to the problems it could pose. This setting is also appropriate for sharing the assumptions and thoughts identified for the risk. During this discussion it is not uncommon to discover additional risks that were not evident before because what the team highlighted depended on the original risk, should it occur. Impact measures the effect it can have on the project. Probability refers to the likelihood of that risk occurring during the length of the project. Rate your risk on a scale of 1 through 10 and multiply the two numbers together. This is the Risk Value. Now you can address the risks with the highest value.

4. *Design*

After identifying the critical risks that loom over your project's success, you need to plan on how you will approach them. This can be an in-depth plan, but sticking to a more agile environment, simplicity is still favored. The wording is important in this step because it can elicit action from team members or stakeholders without directly saying so. Some wording for risks include:

- *25+- Critical-* Urgent action needed, track on a daily basis
- *15-20- Serious-* Monitor over the week, involve management as needed

- *6 -12- Moderate-* Monitor and review each month

- *1-5- Minimal-* Review each quarter, will have little impact on the project should it occur, no action needed

Keep track of each assessment you complete. You should be doing this at the start of a planning session and it's used for only 1 sprint. As each sprint is completed and a new one begins, add to the register so you can see and track the progression through the life of the project. You can also make sure, as the project moves toward completion, your risks are being managed well so your success is not in danger.

5. *Undertake the plan*

When you come up with a strategy to mitigate the risk, you now need to act on that strategy. It may sound simple and intuitive, which it is, but it is a hard step for people to take. Humans are procrastinators, especially if the work before you is hard or not interesting to you. But if you avoid taking action, you are playing "Russian roulette" with your project's success! Part of the success of a risk-averting action plan is that it tackles the most "dangerous" risk first. This way you can rest easy knowing that you did what you could to make the project successful.

Another component of taking action is to make sure that if you need to fail, that you fail early in the process. This does not mean you need to throw in the towel on the project, but it is important to identify the reality of a risk and its potential impact on your process. If it is most likely going to happen and it will cripple your efforts, would you rather know sooner, before a lot of work is put in, or later, when you have poured your heart and efforts into something that will never materialize? If you find that the project is not addressable as it is, you can walk away from the task and do something else, or you can revisit the project,s plan to approach it from another perspective. Sometimes, it can open a dialogue to secure additional resources or different skills on the team to help the project succeed.

6. *Repeat*

Thankfully, repeating is simple and easy to do. When you have experience identifying risks early,creating an actionable plan to mitigate the risks is a key component to a successful project. When you complete these steps correctly, you can appreciate a continual valuable assess-to-act cycle that always shows, manages, and minimizes risks. Make sure you review your risk plan each quarter at the least, but ideally, you should align it with a planning session for the new sprint. These meetings provide access to the complete team who has access to the risks, assessments, and measurements of each. The review does not need to be in great detail for each planning session, but it should reflect the risks on the risk register you have identified as the most important to mitigate next, so the project can have greater opportunity for success. Planning sessions are also good opportunities to find new risks not managed before. This is because as the team works through the project, new challenges may appear, offering new risks that you need to consider. During this process, if you find a risk that scores high and is potentially threatening to the success of the project, you need to make sure to address it quickly.

Thankfully, the process of analyzing the risks facing your agile project is simple. You can simply follow the six steps outlined above to keep an eye on threats to your success and remove the opportunity for failure by being prepared, thanks to your collaboration with the team.

Chapter 13: Final Tips for Having Success with Agile Project Management

If you have made it to the end of this book and are still experiencing failure in your agile projects, do not fear, you are not alone. There is still room for improvement to your process! But maybe what you need is not hidden in the previous pages of this book. Perhaps what you are looking for is listed below in this final chapter.

5 Tips for Success with Agile

1. *Trust should be an atmosphere you create for your team*

As a manager, you need to connect with the stakeholders in the project. Each individual must be open to discussing priorities. This is best done when you give each person the opportunity to speak and be heard, and you respect their input. These simple actions allow your team members and the team to flourish.

2. *Be a good listener for both stakeholders*

A good agile project manager needs to see the project from both sides: the company and the customer. But it also means seeing the project from the view of the team members in the company and the executives. The change to an agile environment can be hard for executives and other stakeholders as well, so make sure you listen to what they are encountering, to help them, too.

3. *Obstacles should be found and removed for your team*

Ask your team often about the barriers they encounter to their success. Find out how they think you can aid them in resolving the issues. For example, if someone does not like to speak in a group setting so does not contribute during daily stand-ups, you need to work together to find a way for them to be heard but not in a public setting. This could be a simple note or email that highlights their contributions and plans for you to be aware of.

4. *Learning is at the center*

The team is not the only group of people you need in your agile corner. This means you need to educate the executive level and mid-level managers as well as any other stakeholder you need on your side. They need to clearly visualize the benefits of changing to agile. Sometimes you need to call in support to sell the idea to the group. This person could give all the details about the process that you may not want to or be able to provide a persuasive argument for.

5. *Mentor*

Sometimes you need mentoring to learn the practices of agile in a successful environment. Instead of blaming a methodology or process, consider taking ownership of your management methods and see if you are the cause of constant failure. You perhaps need a reluctant team member to get on board, so you have them mentored by another enthusiastic and knowledgeable team member. However, if it is you that needs mentoring, find a coach or another team or business that is successful with agile and begin learning all you can from their approach and style.

10 Tips on Becoming an Agile Team

1. *Recognize your role in the process.*

Being agile is a balancing act you will need constant work on. You need to be visionary and team-focused, but you also need to release control and encourage the team to be flexible, open to change and communicate openly and honestly.

2. *Take your first action and keep it going*

New technology and processes are being rolled out, and different roles and terms are being used. People on your team are reading books and blogs to better understand this agile process. But even though you are still exploring the concepts, once you say it is "go" time, you need to make sure that it is full steam ahead! Do not hold back. The best way to get to know a new technology, process, or form is to use it in a real-life setting. You will encounter challenges, but now you have the tools to handle them. Use this fresh new start as a way to clearly define the values of your team and their purpose in the larger picture.

3. *Solve problems that you know about*

Consistent, focused direction is how your team can be successful. To give direction, you need to know what the needs are and find ways to meet them. This practice also requires you to determine if the problem needs to be addressed right away or could wait for another time. A skill you will develop with time is the ability to see a problem, develop a solution, and implement of the plan when the timing is the most advantageous to your customer and the project.

4. *Keep the speed going*

As you chug toward your project completion, you may find you and your team members losing the "steam" of a new project and process. When this occurs, you will find problems in front of you that you will have more difficulty handling. You can model stamina by setting a steady pace for yourself and encouraging others to do the same. Allow team members to share about how they feel the pace is set, and set the tools for their tasks out, so they have what they need when they need it.

Encourage short, 5-minute breaks to decompress when needed, but then push right back into the project at hand to get it done.

5. Minimal planning is necessary

Meetings that you host should give the team the chance to help clarify and identify short-term goals related to the long-term project objective. These goals can then be broken into pieces to help the team complete the tasks and deliver value to the customer. Just make sure you do not spend too much time on the planning part and more time on delivery.

6. Talk to the face

Speaking to someone face-to-face is the best method of communication. You can share an immense amount of information efficiently and it removes uncertainty in your message or tone.

7. Stay motivated

Team members who are motivated will give you quality work. Find team members who are internally driven for success and allow them to take the responsibility of handling the tasks in the manner that they feel is appropriate. This ownership and autonomy will breed motivation and valuable work.

8. Give your team the room to organize themselves

Agile is far from micromanaging. You will not be demanding specific actions or making decisions for them. Now, you are allowing them to determine the best structure for the team to get the job done. Facilitate the process but do not guide or dictate how it will work best.

9. Simple, simple, simple

Anywhere and everywhere you can, make it simple. Simple communication, meetings, plans, processes, metrics. You name it—make it simple.

10. Review work often so it becomes a habit

Your goal is your endpoint. If your actions are not bringing you closer to it, you need to stop and adjust accordingly. The best way to know if you are on target is to pause and review your actions and efforts. Do this often, so you do not waste time going in the wrong direction.

Conclusion

The next step is to set up a meeting with your executives and start the discussion about how agile will fit in with your company. Chances are, because of its versatility, you have already figured out how it will work and why it will benefit your business. Now you need to go get the others on board with you. Show them this book to get their wheels turning, too! The more buy-in and knowledge of whom your company's key players are, the better agile will work on your environment. And with buy-in and knowledge, you get ownership and then more and more success. The habits will be created, and success will become second nature, and you'll be the one to thank for bringing this tool to the table. Congratulations!

When you get those folks on the same page as you, you need to determine what methodology you will use. This can be a trial-and-error period for your company, but try to choose a method outlined in the chapters of this book to help you transition with success to an agile environment. Remember, your new atmosphere will need to "be" agile, not just "do" it. With the right method employed, you will be able to observe the ownership of the teams growing with each project you complete using your visionary agile approach.

If you found this individual book on Agile Project Management useful in any way, can you please leave a review for it?

Thanks for your support!

Part 2: Kanban

The Ultimate Guide to Kanban Methodology for Agile Software Development

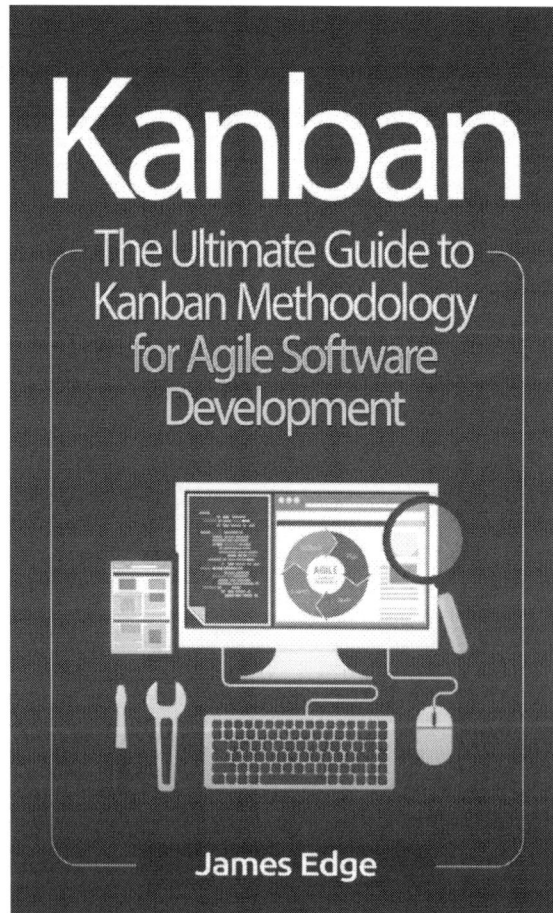

Introduction

You could start to test all different types of methods for project management, but that will take too much time, and can be tedious. Though you may learn a lot from all of your experiments, when it comes down to getting things done, you need to have the most efficient method. You can still use the old standbys of test-driven development, pair programming, and planning poker. A lot of people discovered that Scrum had a huge impact on their productivity; that was, until they found Kanban.

Production teams have found that every minute they use Kanban has added value to their products and for their customers. They don't waste any time or effort, and they know their work is quality work.

This book is here to introduce you to this amazing system. You won't have to do any experiments or go through any mishaps. All you have to do is follow the information and then reap the rewards of the Kanban system. Don't wait and allow your competition to find this information first. Make use of the Kanban system and reap all of the benefits this management system can bring.

What is Kanban?

The Kanban system is a system used to schedule just-in-time manufacturing and lean manufacturing. In Japanese, Kanban literally means billboard or signboard. A Toyota industrial engineer, Taiichi Ohno, came up with Kanban to increase their manufacturing efficiency. The name was derived from the cards the factory used to track production. For those that work in the automotive industry, Kanban is known to all as "Toyota nameplate system." This is the reason why other automobile manufacturers don't want to use the term Kanban.

Kanban immediately became useful in helping support a production system and promoting further improvement. The system is used in finding problem areas by measuring lead times and cycle of the process and its steps. The biggest benefit of Kanban is that it creates upper limits to work in process inventory to prevent overcapacity.

One of the main goals of the system is preventing excess inventory buildup within the production areas. Limits are placed on items stored at supply points. Once inefficiencies are identified, the limits are reduced and then eventually removed. When limits are exceeded, the identified inefficiency will be taken care of.

History

The Kanban system originated from an empty box which was just a simple replenishment signaling system. The UK Spitfire factories first developed this during the war, and they referred to it as the "two-bin system." Then, in the late '40s, Toyota began to search supermarkets to look for shelf-stocking methods to use on their factory floor.

When it comes to grocery stores, customers will typically get what they need at the needed time. Furthermore, customers only take what they need, knowing there will surely be a future supply. This is why grocery stores only stock things expected to sell at a particular time. Noticing this, Toyota started to compare a process to a customer from previous processes, as well as the previous processes to a store.

Kanban is used to align the levels of inventory with consumption. There will be a signal indicating that a specific material was already consumed, and the supplier now needs to deliver a new shipment. The replenishment cycle will track these signals, which will bring visibility to the buyer, supplier, and consumer.

The demand rate is what Kanban uses to control the production rate. The demand is passed from the very last buyer up to the store processes. In 1953, Toyota used this new idea in their machine shop.

Toyota Operations

A demand forecasting needed a push, which is why production scheduling was a success. On the contrary, Kanban approaches by pulling from the demand, before the ordering the product. Production and re-supply will be figured out based on customer orders.

When the supply time becomes too long, and the demand is still uncertain, the best thing to do is to quickly respond when a demand is noticed. The Kanban system excels this way. The Kanban system acts as a demand signal which will quickly make its way to the supply chain. This will ensure better management and smaller amount of the intermediate stock in the supply chain. When the response to supply is slower than the demand fluctuations, which causes a possible lost sale, building of stocks may be appropriately considered. Kanban is then added to the system to reach the required stocks.

Taiichi Ohno explains that for a Kanban system to be effective, it has to follow strict rules. Toyota came up with a list of six rules. They have to constantly monitor those rules, which will ensure that their Kanban system does exactly what it needs to.

The six rules that Toyota formulated for their Kanban application are:

1. All processes will provide a request to its supplier as the supplies are consumed.

2. All processes are produced based upon the sequence and quantity of incoming requests.

3. Without a request, nothing will be made or delivered.

4. The request is always attached to the item.

5. Processes have to ensure that they only deliver defect-free items.

6. Pending requests should be limited to make sure that the processes are sensitive and determine the inefficiencies.

Cards

The Kanban cards help in signaling the movement of the materials as well as in switching materials from the outside supplier to the main production facility, making it a very important part of the Kanban system. This card is like a message showing the depletion of parts, products, or inventory. When Kanban receives the message, it will trigger the replenishment of that particular part, product, or inventory. The consumption will trigger the demand for additional production, while the card will prompt the demand for products. In simpler terms, the Kanban cards produce a system driven by demands.

In terms of lean production proponents, they have always believed that demand-driven systems will lead to lower inventory levels and quicker turnarounds. This ends up helping companies be more competitive by implementing these types of systems.

Systems that use Kanban signals have become increasingly popular over the last couple of years. This new trend has reduced the usage of Kanban cards. However, it is still commonly used in modern production facilities. Kanban uses email notification in signaling demand to the suppliers. It can also be used in various kinds of software systems. A "Kanban trigger" will be activated when a specific part has hit a lower amount than the number that was indicated on the card. It will demand a purchase order with set quantities to the suppliers. The supplier then needs to fulfill the request within the specified time.

While the Kanban cards have stuck to the primary principles of Kanban, it still needs extra materials. There's a need for more parts if an empty bin contains a red card.

Three-Bin System

The simplest example of the Kanban system is the "three-bin system." This is used when there is no in-house manufacturing of supplied parts. Their initial demand point is the bin found on the floor of the factory. The inventory control point is the bin located in the factory store. Finally, the supplier has the last bin. The classic Kanban cards are removable cards found in each bin which contain the details and other important facts about the product.

Since the parts inside the bin positioned on the factory floor are used for manufacturing and are often empty, the bin, along with its Kanban card, is sent to the store. The store will replace the emptied bin with a full one that also has its own Kanban card. The empty bin will then be sent out to the supplier from the factory store.

The supplier will eventually give its product bin with card back to the factory store. The empty bin is now at the supplier. This is the final step in the process, meaning it will never run out of the product. It can also be considered a closed-loop process. This is because it only provides the exact amount of the product needed in a single bin without worrying about oversupply. The spare bin will allow for any uncertainties in supply, transport, and use. The best system will compute enough Kanban cards for each product. The heijunka box, a colored-board system, is commonly used in many major factories.

Electronic

Several manufacturers have started to use an electronic Kanban system, which will help to reduce the common problems like lost cards and manual entry errors. Electronic systems can be used in enterprise resource planning systems, which will enable real-time demand signals throughout the supply chain as well as improve the visibility. Tracking the supplier leads and the replenishment times from the date taken from the electronic system can improve the levels of the inventory.

Functioning as a signaling system, the Electronic Kanban uses a combination of technology in triggering the movement of the materials, both in the manufacturing and production. The use of technology such as barcodes differentiates this kind of Kanban from the original, which still uses cards and email messages.

Inventory is typically marked with barcodes, which a worker uses at the process' various stages to signal usage. Messages are sent out through the scans to the external and internal stores to ensure that the products are restocked. The messages are routed to the suppliers through the internet. The inventory can also be viewed in real time.

Organizations like Bombardier Aerospace and Ford Motor Company have improved their processes using electronic Kanban systems. You can see widespread use of these systems from bolt-on modules or single solutions to ERP systems.

Systems

Adjacent upstream and downstream workstations talk to each other within the Kanban system through their cards, where all bins have an associated Kanban. An important part of this is Economic Order Quantity. The more popular types of Kanban systems are:

- Transportation Kanban – This authorizes the transport of a full bin to a workstation downstream. This is also found in the bins that are connected to the transportation to move throughout the loop again.

- Production Kanban – Once received, this Kanban authorizes a station to make a definite number of products. The containers associated with it carry this Kanban.

Kanban and Software Development

You know how Kanban got started, and how it was meant to be used. Now, let's look at how it can be helpful in software development. Let's begin by looking at the differences in the planning process between different agile methodologies.

Differences between Scrum and the Kanban methodology:

- Kanban contains no timeboxes at all.

- Kanban methodology tasks are larger, and there are fewer tasks.

- It's optional to use periodical assessments in Kanban, or there aren't any at all.

- Kanban has no "speed of team." They only have an average time for full implementation.

Looking at this list, think about what will remain of the agile methodology if sprints are taken out, dimensions are increased, and you stop counting the speed of your team's work. What remains? Nothing?

How would you be able to talk about any supervision over development if you get rid of all the major tools?

Managers like to think they have to be in control all the time. Their supervision over the development process doesn't exist. If a team isn't interested in working, it is going to fail a project despite any control level.

If a team enjoys their work and works with complete efficiency, then you don't need control. The control will only disturb the process and increase the cost.

For example, one of the most common problems with Scrum is the higher costs because of discussions, meetings, and time lost at the joints of the sprints. At the very least, a day is used to complete a sprint, and another to begin another sprint. If you have a two-week sprint, then two days out of those two weeks comes to 20%, which is a lot of wasted time. So when you use Srum methodology, around 30% to 40% of the time will be wasted on supporting the process, which includes daily rallies, sprint retrospectives, and on and on.

Kanban differs because it focuses on the task. When a team uses Scrum, their main objective is successfully completing the sprint. Tasks take first place in the Kanban methodology. You don't have sprints, and a single team works on a task from start to finish. Deployment will then be made when it is ready, based on the presentation of the work that has been done. The Kanban team doesn't estimate time to finish a task since it doesn't make any sense, and it's almost always wrong.

Why would a manager have to have a time estimate if they fully believe in their team's ability? Their team will work off of a Kanban board, which we will talk more in depth about later. On the board, columns to be read from left to right, may contain information like:

- Goals – This is an optional column for a board. Goals that are high-level can be added here so that everybody on the team knows about them and is easily reminded of them. Some example goals could be "Add Windows 10 support" or "20% increase of work speed."

- Story Queue – This is where all of the tasks that are ready to be started should be placed. The one with the highest priority is placed at the top and is taken first. The card is then moved to the next column.

- Acceptance and Elaboration – This column, along with all of the other columns before "Done," will vary based upon the workflow of certain teams. Tasks that are under discussion can be added here. Once you finish your discussion, you can move the task to the next column.

- Development – This is where a task will remain until the development of the feature has been completed. Once you finish the task, it will be moved into the next column. If it turns out the architecture is uncertain or incorrect, you can move it back a column.

- Test – This is where a task lives when it is being tested. Once it has been successfully tested, it is moved into the next column. If any issues come up, then the task should be shifted back to the development phase.

- Deployment – Every project will have its own deployment. This column could mean that you put a new version on the server, or you commit the code to the repository.

- Done – The card will move to this column once it has made it through every other section on the board, and it is completely finished.

When teams use Kanban for software development, work is pulled as capacity permits. Work is never pushed into the process. This system aids in the decision-making about how much, what, and when to produce something.

The organization of a Kanban board allows for a better understanding of the workflow. It reduces waste from multitasking and context switching, shows all of the operational problems, and helps with collaboration to improve the system.

The diagrams in this book show typical Kanban board sections for workflow. The boards will vary considerably depending on the context in which they are used. The overall aim is to make the workflow and progress of individual items clear to the stakeholders and participants.

Some of the biggest companies use a Kanban system to improve their work. For example, Pixar's creative process has been heavily influenced by a Kanban system.

The President of Pixar Animation, Ed Catmull, feels it is important that their animations be made in order. This means that every team passes the product, or idea, on to the following team who will push it further down the board.

They use high-level Kanban boards to make sure that this happens. The staff that is working on a production knows exactly what they are supposed to be doing, and how their work affects their colleagues.

Spotify has also started to use a Kanban system. When it came to the Kanban board, the operations team wanted to make it as easy as possible. They have three sections: to-do, doing, done.

Their board also has two horizontal lanes. All tangible tasks, like 'upgrading data storage' are placed here, while the other lane is made up of intangible work like 'designing databases' and 'planning a server migration.'

Spotify switched to a Kanban system once they realized their workload was reactive instead of proactive. This meant that it struggled to find the time for planned projects.

They section their work into small, medium, or large tasks. The small tasks take a day, medium ones a few days, and large jobs take a week. Tasks that take longer than a week are called projects. They then split those projects up into small, medium, and large tasks. They can then place them into the backlog.

Kanban Benefits

In the early 2000s, business leaders became interested in Kanban when it was mainly used by software developers to improve workflow. Today, it has started to be used across all disciplines to help teams visualize, optimize, and manage their work.

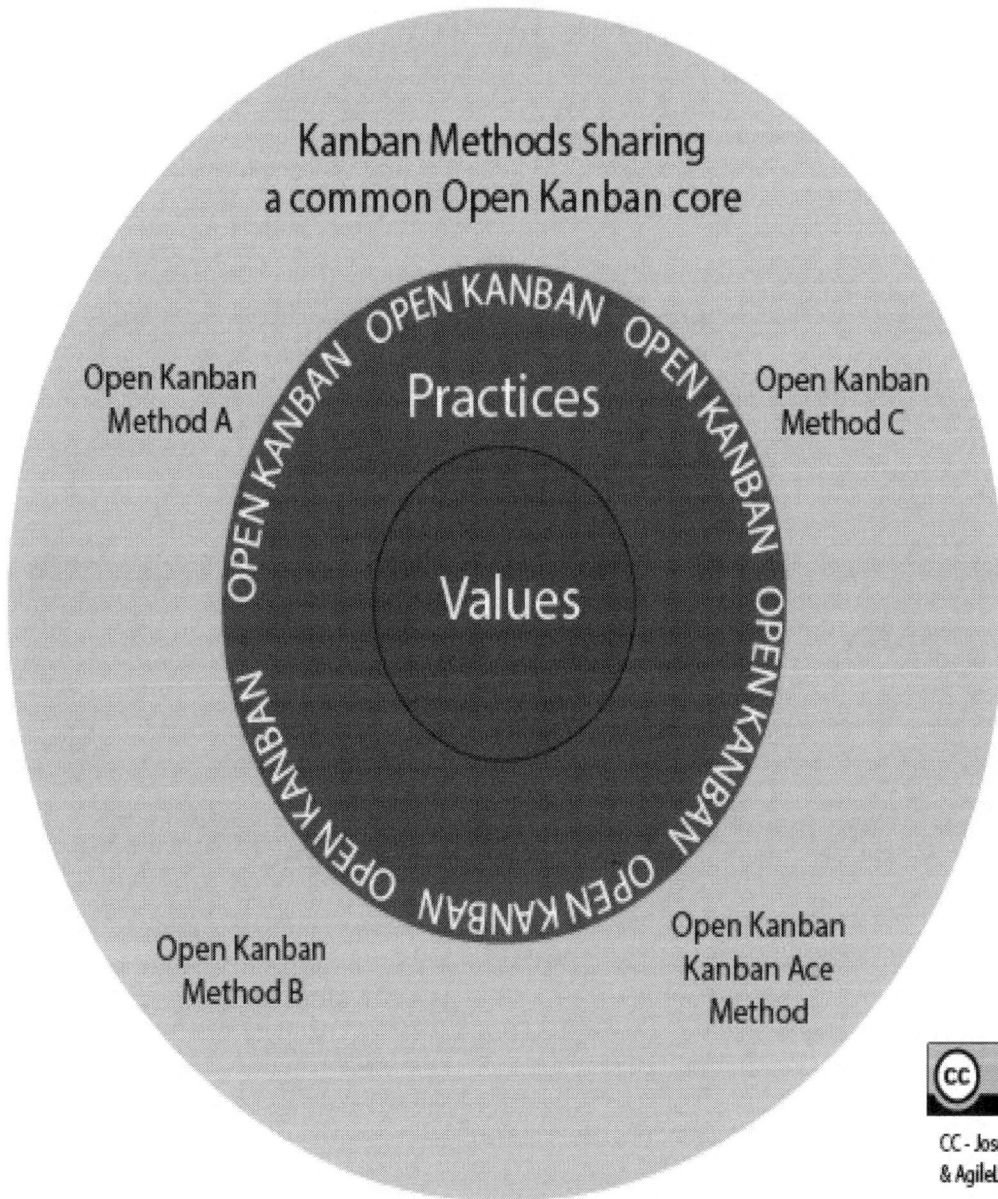

Kanban Methods Sharing
a common Open Kanban core

OPEN KANBAN

Practices

Values

Open Kanban
Method A

Open Kanban
Method C

Open Kanban
Method B

Open Kanban
Kanban Ace
Method

Even science agreed on the benefits of Kanban. Visual information can be processed by the brain 60,000 times quicker than with words. Kanban kicks understanding and communication, by using visual information, into high gear.

Let's look at the several benefits your team can reap from using Kanban.

1. Versatility

The main point behind the Kanban system is communication with the use of visual signals. This benefits industries and job titles everywhere. Kanban can be applied anywhere. Any company can use Kanban either from marketing department or engineering. It's easier for projects and team members to smoothly move through various functions because of Kanban's versatility. An example of it is when moving content project to graphics from editing, or a new feature to testing from integration.

2. Continuous Improvement

Kanban's main principle encourages people to focus more on continuous improvement. Reviewing process is a lot easier due to the project management's visual system, as well as making necessary improvements to streamline workflow, remove the waste, and reduce overhead.

3. Responsiveness

Within the auto industry, where Kanban got its start, it uses process when low in inventory, creating a better method of matching demand and inventory. When used in project management, responsiveness is still a huge benefit of Kanban. With Kanban, responding to business needs in a more agile way is much easier.

4. Increased Output

The team can limit the work in progress, called limiting "WIP," using the Kanban system. Doing this, the teams are encouraged to work closely with each other in removing distractions, and multitask to finish their work. The teams can get more things done because of the improvement in intense focus and collaboration. With a more focused delivery, high-priority and high-value work items are expedited while delivering value to the business. Personal WIP limits help to relieve teams from overburdening because they can focus on a finite number of work items. They only move on to.the next item in the input queue when the item that they were originally committed to is completely finished.

5. Empowered Teams

The whole team is in control of the Kanban system, and they share responsibilities for finishing the work. Kanban helps to empower the team to make agile decisions that move the project forward with efficiency and innovation. The typical siloed organizations that battle between product management and software delivery, become more integrated into the development value stream. Kanban encourages synergy between groups and helps to break down the walls between different specializations, which results in collaboration between functions. Work item transitions between columns on the board will offer opportunities for communication, collaboration, knowledge discovery, and involvement and engagement for all.

6. A Perfect Product

Projects typically make their way to the finish line with fewer reworks and errors because of the increased concentration on continuous improvement and quick-response. Quality control can now be allowed in the project management in order to give more accurate results. Looking at it from a nontechnical perspective, there are lots of activities that contribute to high-quality software, like collaborative analysis and user documentation. Even within disciplined teams, the collective behavior is controlled by rules. The policies will help to solidify the professional standards that are agreed on across the board, which includes software teams, product and project managers, and stakeholders.

7. Business Value First

Kanban is positioned to be a decisions management framework, which makes it a lot more powerful than it looks from an outsider's view. It isn't just some board hung up on the wall! It helps to promote economically-based decision-making by managing and prioritizing work based on certain economic goals. Organizations are trying to survive in fiercely competitive environments. This means that we need to execute, identify, and prioritize the most valuable work so that the business can keep afloat and ahead of the competition.

8. Visibility

An amazing thing about most organizations is the amount of work that happens under the parapet. One of the core practices of Kanban is to make invisible work visible! By using a Kanban board as an information center, as well as its other merits, it offers a holistic view of process inefficiencies, blockers, impediments, bottlenecks, and progress at one glance. Information can be easily found by not only the team members but by the external observers and stakeholders. This promotes a boundaryless flow of information across the entire organization.

9. Reduction of Wasteful Activities

The majority of project managers will focus most on the timeline instead of process queues. Timelines are a part of the manager's psyche, along with Gantt charts, spreadsheets, and other time-bound documents. They don't like to embrace uncertainty. With the reinforcement of WIP limits, a Kanban board turns into a pull-based system, which keeps a reliable amount of high-quality ideas that are delivered JIT (Just In Time), while getting rid of wasteful work and lower queues. Upstream activities like business cases, discovery workshops, and requirements gathering, take place on demand and when they have to, which forces the team to make timely decisions.

10. Sustainability

Kanban systems help to manage your work at a sustainable, smooth, and humane pace, without any uncontrollable nadirs and distressing peaks, which only causes frustration, high employee turnover, and lack of commitment. A sustainable development brings about creativity, as WIP limits help to control the pace dynamically without fear of breaking a promise down the road. This allows for innovation, addresses issues in a new way, and produces solutions with fewer issues in quality.

Kanban and Lean

During the last 20 years, Kanban, Scrum, Lean, and Agile have been steadily gaining in popularity in different industries and fields.

The Project Management Institute stated that 75% of organizations that were agile were able to meet their goals or business intent with 65% finishing on time, and 67% finishing on budget. This is higher than those organizations with low agility. In the same research study, agile organizations' revenue grew 37% faster and generated 330% more profits than non-agile companies.

Lean principles have also proven that they are effective. Thanks to using a lean approach, Dropbox was able to go from 100,000 registered users to more than four million in only 15 months. The Wealthfront Company now manages more than two hundred million dollars and processes more than two million dollars on a given day. IMVU has managed to reach 50 million registered users and now makes over forty million dollars annually.

While a lot of companies have started to implement or are leaning towards these methodologies, there is typically only a handful of people in the company who actually understand the entire process.

Other employees, especially when it comes to big companies with difficult communication, follow along with the rules without a lot of deep insight. This does not mean that they aren't good at what they do—it might even be the opposite—they could be more focused on their functional tasks.

The Agile Pyramid

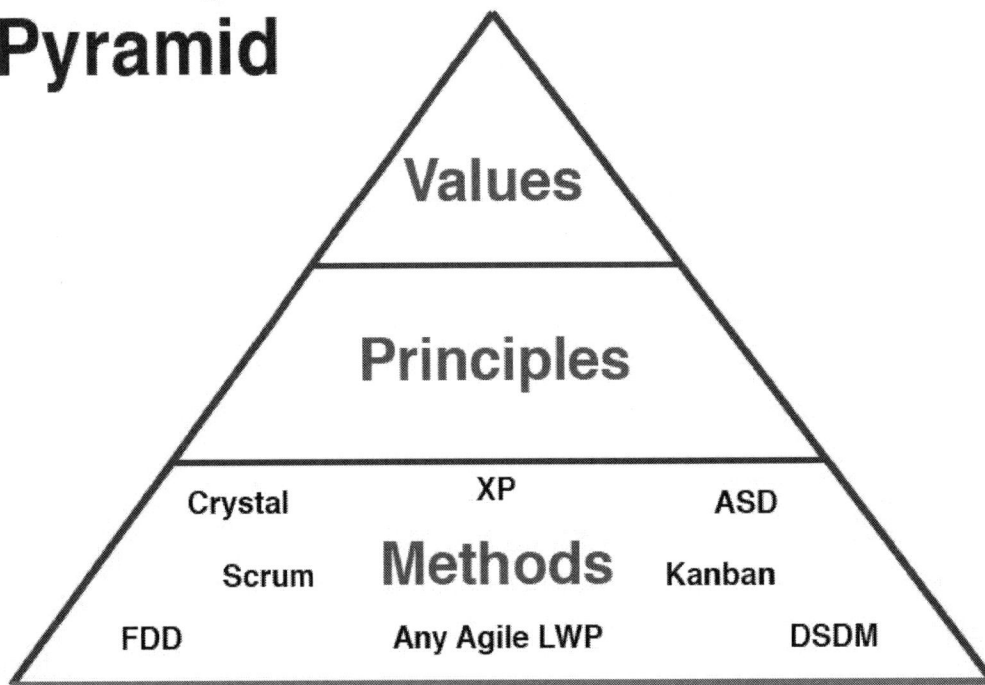

Values

Principles

Crystal   XP   ASD

Scrum   **Methods**   Kanban

FDD   Any Agile LWP   DSDM

But while they aren't aware of the basic principles, don't share the corporate philosophy, aren't ready to challenge another, or can't see the difference between Scrum and Kanban, Agile and Lean, the company isn't going to see any change in their productivity.

So how are these things different and similar? Let's see.

Agile

In 2001, Agile was officially born from the Agile Manifesto to help improve productivity in software development. But it has started to expand to other areas. A project team that chooses to follow the 12 Agile principles is considered agile. Basically, agile is time-focused and an iterative philosophy that lets a team build a produce incrementally, and deliver it in small pieces. The biggest benefit is the ability to change and adapt at any point along the way depending on corporate obstacles, market conditions, feedback, and so on. They only supply relevant products to the market.

This is the reason why an agile company tends to be flexible, adapts to changes quickly, iterates less while they implement faster, and can seize new chances as they come up. It helps to provide them with a fast decision-making process by using a flexible organizational structure and basic communication. In 2015, research among 601 IT and development professionals showed that agile is the main approach for management. And it is mainly used to enhance collaboration and improve software quality.

Lean

Lean, along with Kanban, got its start in the mid-'50s in Japan within their automotive industry. Its main purpose was to reduce loss and create a sustainable production. Lean was adapted for use in software development in the 2000s by Tom and Mary Poppendiecks who connected it to the seven initial Lean principles and Agile philosophy.

Following along with expanding Lean to any industry, Eric Reis applied it to the start-up industry in 2008 in order to help develop new services and products in times of uncertainty. In order for a start-up to be considered Lean, they have to follow the five Lean principles created by Eric Reis.

The typical Lean company will follow a 'learn, measure, build' cycle. They will do several tests, frequently connect with their customers, understand their value, and look at its key processes to make continuous improvements. By using this never-ending cycle, a start-up will become sustainable, develop smartly, and have success. By lowering the high cost of trying to get the first customer and the even bigger cost of making the wrong product, and decreasing the technology development cycles, the Lean start-up philosophy will help new ventures to launch products that their customers will actually be interested in. This enables things to be done more quickly and at a lower cost than traditional methods, which makes start-ups less risky.

As can easily be seen, both Lean and Agile aim at achieving business goals and making their client happy with a product of the best quality. These, as well as several other shared features between these mindsets, will typically lead people to confuse the two. However, they work with different tasks and purposes, and that's the reason why it is important to create a clear line between the two.

Agile and Lean aren't methodologies. They are principles that create the basis for many different methodologies, so they are more of a mindset or philosophy.

Lean is a wider-known term than Agile because its smart approach improves all types of losses like energy, labor, and money. Jeff Sutherland also explains that Agile was created after Lean, so that means that they are closely related. Conceptually, Agile is actually a subset of Lean practices and principles, which are actually a subset of Systems Thinking.

This means that Kanban is a methodology. Kanban is a part of the Lean philosophy supported by the Japanese automotive industry. But the trick is, you can still see Agile principles within the Kanban methodology.

Kanban Goals

When using a Kanban system, you will have to come up with primary and secondary goals. These are things you will have arrive at on your own, but here are some things you should strive for.

    1. Primary Goal: Better performance with process improvements that are introduced with little resistance.

Your team is likely using Kanban because you believe that it will provide a better way to introduce change. Kanban is there to change as little as it has to, so that means change with very little resistance would be the first goal.

    2. Secondary Goal: Deliver with high quality.

As you know, Kanban can help you deliver every element of the recipe for success. Kanban will help you focus on the quality of your product by limiting work in 0progress. It will allow you to define policies around what you find acceptable before you can pull a work item to the next step. You can include quality criteria with these policies. For example, we could set a strict policy that you can't pull user stories into test until the other tests have passed and their bugs have been resolved. This means that we are stopping the line until the story is in the right condition to continue.

    3. Secondary Goal: Control the quantity of WIP to deliver a predictable cycle time.

We all know that work-in-progress is directly connected to the cycle time and that you can find a correlation between non-linear growth and time-in defect rates. It makes complete sense that WIP needs to be kept small. It will make everybody's life easier if we agree to limit this to a certain quantity. This will end up making cycle times dependable, to an extent, and will help to keep lower defect rates.

    4. Secondary Goal: Allow the team members to have a better life by improving work/life balance.

While most companies talk a lot about employee satisfaction, it is very seldom a priority. Senior managers and investors too, easily view resources as fungible and easily replaced. This shows where there is a cost-centric bias in their investment or management approach. They don't look at the huge impact on performance that comes along with an experienced and well-motivated team.

Staff retention is extremely important for work. As software developers age, they start to care more about the rest of their lives. A lot of them lament about how they wasted their 20s away slaving in their office over a piece of code that didn't reach expectations.

When it comes to work/life balance, it's not just balancing the number of hours a person spends at work with how many hours they get with their family and hobbies. It also has to do with providing reliability. For example, let's say that you have a team member who enjoys art and wants to take a painting class. This is every Wednesday starting at 6:30, and runs for ten weeks. Is your team able to provide that person with the certainty that they will be able to leave the office on time every Wednesday to go to that class?

When you give your team the right kind of work/life balance, your company will appear more attractive to the local market. It gives your employees motivation, and it provides your team with energy to maintain high-performance levels for months or years. It's not true that you get the best performance from knowledgeable workers being overloaded with work. This might work in a tactical sense for a few days, but it is not going to be sustainable beyond a few weeks. It's just good business to give your team a good work/life balance by not overloading them with too much work.

> 5. Secondary Goal: Give your team slack by keeping a balance between demand and throughput.

While balanced demand with throughput can be used to avoid overworking your team and gives them a good work/life balance, it also causes something else. It creates slack in the value chain. Every value chain has a bottleneck. The throughput that you provide downstream is limited by the throughput of your bottleneck, no matter how far upstream it was. That means, when you balance the input demand with your throughput, you will make idle time throughout your value chain except for the bottleneck resources.

The majority of managers steer clear of idle time. They have been trained to manage for efficiency, and it feels as if changes could be made to lower costs when there is idle time. This might be true, but you also need to appreciate the power of slack.

Slack can help responsiveness to the urgent requests, and it provides bandwidth to facilitate process improvements. If you don't have any slack, team members won't be able to take the time to reflect on how their work is done and how it could be better. Without slack, they won't have time to learn more techniques that will help to improve their tooling or skills. Without slack, you won't have any liquidity in your system, so that you can respond to late changes or urgent requests. You won't have any tactical agility without slack.

> 6. Secondary Goal: Use a simple prioritization mechanism that slows commitment and keeps your options open.

After the previous goals have been achieved, you will have created an engine for making software. After you have this in place, it's important that you make use of it. This requires that you have a prioritization method that will maximize your value, and it will minimize your cost and risk. You need a prioritization scheme that will optimize your business performance.

A lot of schemes are simple, like "high, medium, low." This type of scheme doesn't have direct meaning for the business. The more elaborate schemes started once Agile software had developed things like MoSCoW: "Must have, Should have, Could have, Won't have." Things like feature-driven development used a simplified and modified version of Kano analysis techniques. Still, others prefer a strict numerical order for value and risk.

These schemes have the same problem. To respond to market change, you have to reprioritize. With the uncertainty of the market, it's hard to predict how things will change.

This is why you need a scheme that will delay commitments as late as possible and give you an easy question to answer. Kanban will give you this by having business owners refill empty queue slots, while they also provide reliable cycle times and due-date performance.

Now, six goals would be enough for many, but here you will get two extra goals to make sure that your Kanban system works at its peak performance.

> 7. Secondary Goal: Have a transparent scheme so that you can see improvement opportunities to enable change to a collaborative culture which will encourage continuous improvement.

When you provide transparency in the WIP, delivery rate, and quality it will build trust with your senior management and customers. This means you provide transparency in every area of the system when something may be finished, the quality, and how well your team works. This gives your customers confidence in your work.

Not only does it put your customers' and senior management's mind at ease, but it also provides something else. Having transparency in the process will allow everybody involved to see the effects of their work. This makes your team more reasonable-minded. Their behavior changes to improve the performance of the system.

> 8. Secondary Goal: Have a process that allows for high-maturity development, good governance, business agility, and predictable results.

Business leaders want to make promises to colleagues at the executive table, to shareholders, to the board of directors, to customers, and the market. They also want to be able to keep those promises.

They also know that the world is fast-paced and there will be changes. That means, they want to be able to respond to those changes quickly and take advantage of all of the opportunities. In order to achieve everything that business leaders want, there needs to be more transparency.

This all comes down to an organization operating at a maturity level of four on the Software Engineering Institute's five-point scale of maturity and capability. There are not very many organizations that have reached this maturity level, regardless of whether they have reached out for an actual SCAMPI appraisal or not. It's no wonder that the majority of senior leaders of the big tech companies are frustrated with their software team's performance.

Step-by-Step Guide

In order to get started with Kanban, all you have to start with is a large board that your entire team can see, and cards to pin on it. But we're going to look at the different areas of a Kanban system so you can better understand how it works. The next chapter will get into the nitty-gritty of making a board.

Project Management

Kanban has been modified to be used in software development in a more project management approach. With the use of Kanban in software development, continuous workflow, which is also known as value stream, can be supported.

- Value Stream: All actions needed to form a project and finish it are included here. The actions can:

    o Give the project value

    o Help to avoid waste

    o Help circumvent non-valuable information.

- Waste Elimination: This is anything that doesn't add value to your project. A Kanban system works to eliminate waste. When it comes to software development, you can have three types of waste:

    o Waste in the potential of the team

    o Waste in project management

    o Waste in code development

- Code development waste happens typically because of:

    o Partially completed work: The work that is partially completed ends up becoming unusable and outdated. This can be eliminated with modular code and iterative cycles that are completed within iterations.

    o Defects: When you are developing code, correction and retesting is absolutely necessary, and it requires resources and time. This can be removed with an updated test suite, continuous customer feedback, and completing testing during the iteration.

- Project management waste happens typically because of:

    o Extra Processes: This is unnecessary documentation that will take resources and time. This could be gotten rid of with:

        ▪ Reviews of documentation that will make sure only necessary and relevant processes are followed

        ▪ Preplanning of all the necessary and relevant processes

    o Code Handoffs: This means that you pass the work between different people or teams after the first person has completed their work. This could cause a lack of knowledge. You can eliminate it by keeping your wireframes and flowcharts clear and visible.

    o Extra Functions: These include the features that aren't needed by the customer. Time and effort will be wasted when you work to develop the functions that are needed for implemented features that the customer hasn't even asked for. This can be removed through continuous communication with your testers and customer involved in the gathering of the requirements. The reason is that they may visualize scenarios better, as well as the expected system behavior.

- Team potential waste happens typically because of:

    o Task Switching: This can cause waste because of multitasking. This can be removed by concentrating on only one task with each release. The larger projects are broken down into tasks to:

    - Give a way to notice and resolve bottlenecks

    - Focus on delivered work-cycle time

    - Enable easy flow of work

    - Reduce dependencies

    - Improve visibility

    o Waiting: This is time wasted for getting information or instructions. The team is subjected to sit idly if they are not enabled to make decisions, or if the team is provided with information that takes expensive resources. This can be eliminated by letting the members of the team:

    - Make decisions in order to prevent them from having to wait for more instructions

    - Have full access to the information they need whenever they need it.

Planning Flexibility

By using Kanban, you will see improvements in your flow of work. Since you will have a visual representation of the workflow, you will notice a reduction in speed from moving one task to another. This is can be done by creating clearly marked Kanban cards, flow lanes, and clearly named columns that show the location of every item within the workflow. A task with longer duration to finish can be done without much hindrance. During this time, the tasks that are finished will continue on to the next step.

This will allow for:

- The right amount of time for longer tasks that you can't logically break down.

- Value preservation for those longer tasks.

- The effort needed for every role can be expended.

- Finished tasks can flow continuously without wasting time.

This makes planning more flexible. It will not also be boxed in.

Pull Approach

When the first team of your two teams shows better performance than the other, it probably pushes more work which is too much to handle for the other team. This can create friction between the two teams. You have to create a pull approach in order to fix this.

The pull approach can remedy this. When the team is ready to work on a project, that is the only time they can pull work. You implement a pull approach by supplying a safeguard with a limited capacity between your teams.

The primary benefits of this kind of approach are:

- Reduces wait times

- Avoids work being piled up

- Helps a team to keep a constant pace and focus on quality

- Gives resource balancing

Minimize Cycle Time

The cycle time of every task is measured, and its process is then optimized in order to reduce the cycle time.

- You will immediately identify the bottlenecks and resolve them in a collaborative manner with the team.

- To reduce having to rework things, correction loops should be considered.

Continuous Delivery

The best things that come from continuous delivery are:

- Your growing products can be delivered continuously at regular times because of short release cycles

- You will have continuous interactions with your customers.

  o This helps you understand what the customers want.

  o It keeps you from producing what a customer doesn't need.

  o You get feedback on modules delivered.

- Every release cycle has limited requirements.

  o Developers don't become overloaded with various requests. This allows them to concentrate more on delivery.

  o You won't have any half-finished work.

- Instead of starting work, the main goal is getting the work finished.
    - This will keep the aim toward providing pace and quality of your product.
    - You can send the product before the customer ends up changing their mind.
- Your workflow will be optimized from start to finish.
    - This will help in incremental process improvements.

Visual Metrics

Having your workflow visualized on a Kanban board will help:

- Schedule following the limits of your WIP on a workflow state.

- Assign your resources in a dynamic way based on the role requirements.

- Continually track progress and status.

Every day, and with every column, mark down how many tasks you have in them. This will give you a chart that looks like a mountain. This chart will give you the performances of the past and will let you predict future results.

This chart will give you information such as:

- The cycle time for every feature by showing the begin date and the end date.

- You can assess the quality of your growing product from a user, technical, and functional perspective at different times.

- The pace of the development can be monitored by observing the amount of completed development items and looking at each item's average time.

- You can adjust the pace of the development by computing the ratio between the development days of each completed item. This ratio can be used to guess the time of completion for items that haven't been developed, and you can adjust the plan as you need to.

- Using a collaborative session, you can adjust and evaluate the process to find the needed changes that could help to improve the quality of the product or to help the development pace.

- Resolve and identify any decisions that are not validated by looking for validated decisions' cycle times. Focus then on fixing loops that are usually the backed-up column you can't see.

Focus and Efficiency

When you focus on your costumers' demands, the scope will become clear. The aim will be on giving the customer value.

Here is how efficiency can be achieved:

- Through continuous customer interactions, their expectations can be made focused and realistic.

- WIP makes sure that tasks are focused on.

- Using a pull approach will enable resources to finish a task at hand before a new task is ever started.

- There will be faster delivery by optimizing lead times.

- By visualizing the workflow with a board, you will draw immediate attention to bottlenecks so that you can quickly fix them.

- The team becomes accountable for their success through empowerment.

Tools

There are lots of different project management tools that use a Kanban approach. Here are just a few you can choose from:

- Kanban Tool: This uses Kanban cards, due dates, tags, swim lanes, and colors to create a Kanban board. The best features include:

  o To-do lists

  o Drag and drop tasks

  o Online documents

  o Visual project management

  o Insightful analytics

  o Online Kanban boards

- Kanbanery: This is another tool that helps your team to work more effectively together through:

  o Real-time updates

  o Work with existing systems

  o Content-rich tasks

  o Advanced reporting

- API and several third-party apps

- iPhone and iPad apps

- Copying or creating task boards with templates

- GitHub integration

• LeanKit: This tool will be helpful in a distributed environment. This can also allow access to the company's CEO, partners, customers, and to all employees.

• JIRA Software: This is an Agile tool that is created for teams of every size and shape. It has features that help with:

- Integrated workflow

- Add-ons

- Workflow

- Reporting

- Releasing

- Tracking

- Value-driven prioritization

- Accurate estimations

- Planning

• Earliz: This software supports smart project collaboration and management.

• Targetprocess: This tool helps manage and visualize Agile projects with the natural and full support of Kanban, Scrum, or custom Agile method. Its features include:

- Visualization of project data

- Visibility of progress

- Test case management

- Custom views, dashboards, reports and cards

- Backlog story map view

- REST

- iOS and Android apps

Kanban Board

There are lots of people who are starting to use a Kanban work management methodology to help visualize their workflow, whether for personal task lists or projects at work. Kanban allows teams and individuals to manage multiple projects and a task by displaying tasks on what is known as a Kanban board. With a traditional board, the tasks will move from left to right as you work toward finishing the project. Ultimately, the use of a Kanban board, especially an online one, will allow teams to stay up to date on overall project progress and task status.

This is extremely useful for teams and individuals who are looking for a visual way to manage tasks and keep the workflow process streamlined and simple. This chapter will dive further into the methodology and mechanics of using an effective Kanban board. We will also look at using two tools to create such a board: Smartsheet and Trello.

The cornerstone of the Kanban methodology is a Kanban board. It is used to help you visualize and track the work that needs to be done. It works like an information hub on all task progress and status. Since you can see all of your tasks on one Kanban board, it functions as a high-level overview of the work. This will end up helping you notice any setbacks or roadblocks and will let the team adapt as they need to.

There are a few key differences in how a Kanban board and a Scrum board work. First off, you won't have to come up with structured sprints for your tasks when you use a Kanban board as you must for a Scrum board. This means, there won't be any need to reset your Kanban board after each completed phase of a task. Instead, you will use the Kanban board for the entire duration of your project or for ongoing work as you receive new tasks.

How is a Board Used?

The best thing about a Kanban board is that it is super simple to set up and intuitive to use. The board setup is very standardized. Of course, you also have the option to customize your Kanban board so that it reflects your project's needs, but sticking to the standard Kanban board structure will help you get things started.

At the very minimum, the Kanban board will have the following three columns organized from left to right:

o Backlog – This is the column where you will place all of the upcoming work. This is where tasks that haven't been started will be stored.

o Work in Progress – This is all of the tasks that are currently being worked on. It's important that you stay under your determined WIP limits (covered later) to make sure that you don't end up overloading yourself or your team with work that is unrealistic to finish in a given time.

o Completed – This is where all of the finished tasks will be placed.

All of your tasks will be placed on a card, and you will move these cards into your various columns as they make it through different phases of the work process. The main goal is that your task will always move from left to right. When you make this a priority, it will make sure that all of your work is fully completed before you go to the next step. This way, it will improve your efficiency.

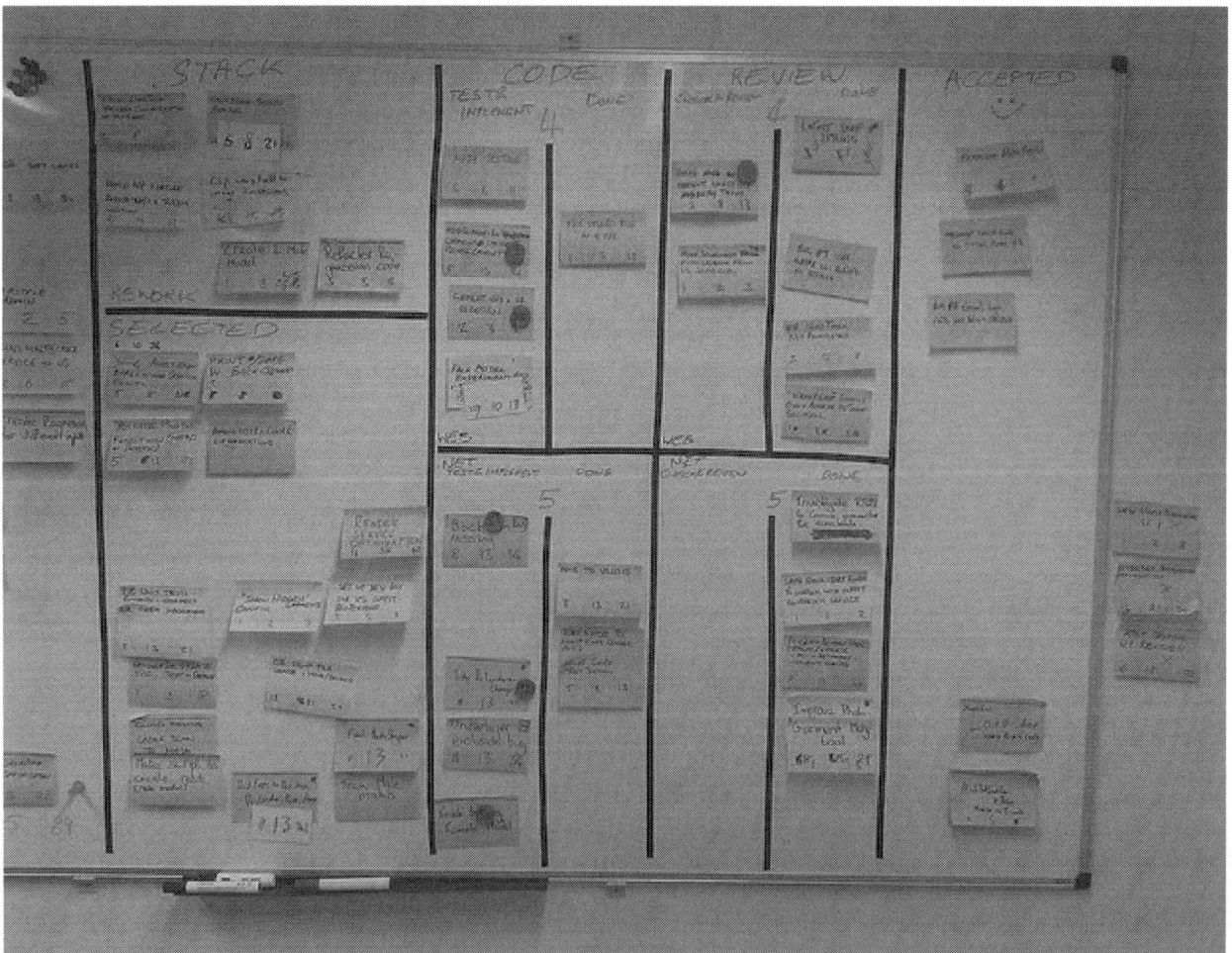

To make things easy for you to get started with Kanban, you can find a lot of different online tools that will help you to make a Kanban board. Two of the most popular tools are Smartsheet and Trello. Trello is a task management tool that will let users come up with task lists and monitor their progress using a Trello board, which can be created and used like a Kanban board. Smartsheet is a web app that can be used like a Kanban board and is great for projects that are more complex.

Trello

The interface of Trello works very similarly to a regular Kanban board. You will create columns to reflect your task status, and you will move the tasks across all of the columns as you get things done.

To get things going using Kanban in Trello, you need to make your first board from scratch.

1. Select the + tab button in the upper right-hand corner to start your blank board. Now, you can create a name for your board.

2. Now, you can make your columns by typing in a column header into the 'Add a list' field that they provide. Here you can create as many columns as you want to, but you do need to create a minimum of at least three: Backlog, In Progress, and Finished.

3. Now you need to add a card to your first column by selecting add a card. Then you will type in the task in the provided field. You can either write out the basic task, or you can write in more detail. This could be due date, labels, or members. You do this by selecting the pencil icon and editing the associated tab.

   a. Labels will let you color-code your tasks if want to help to organize them even further. They also have a colorblind friendly mode that will add texture to your cards.

Strategies International LLC

Kanban Card

QTY

Picture of Item
Here

Card #

Lead Time

Est. Cost- $

Part # -

Supplier Suggestion

Item Description -

Consuming Location-

b. You can choose 'Change members' to assign tasks to certain members.

c. You can choose 'Change due date' to give a task a due date.

d. You can also select copy or move the task into different lanes or columns.

e. To get a more comprehensive menu of how you can edit your card, you can click directly onto the card.

4. Now, you can repeat the previous steps and finish filling-in your task board with the rest of your tasks. You can add a card into any column directly.

5. Once you have your board setup, you will start to move the cards throughout the board. You can drag and drop to move your cards along the board as you finish your work.

6. Remember, you need to make sure that tasks are completely done before you move them into the next column. This will make sure that you don't have to double back on tasks and send them back to a previous column.

There are also additional features when using Trello. For more ways to customize your Kanban board, you can also buy Power-Ups. These are extra features and integrations that will give you even more power. Select the 'Power-Ups' button under the Menu, and you will see things like voting, card again, and calendar.

Calendar will give you an extra calendar view to see your tasks, which can be used weekly or monthly.

Card aging will age your card that you haven't acted upon recently. Once you have actively used the card, the card will be restored to normal vision. This is extremely helpful to ensure that there isn't a task that gets overlooked or continually shoved back.

Voting power-up will let the other users vote on task cards to figure out their priority or interest.

You can also set WIP limits using power-ups, which will give you the opportunity to set a limit on how many tasks can be place in the "In Progress" column. This is an automated way to ensure that you never over-commit yourself or others.

Now you are ready to share your board with the other members of your team.

1. In the upper left-hand corner, you will find a 'Private' button. The sheet will automatically set to private where only you can see it, but it can be shared with several team members, or make it public.

2. Select 'Private' and then pick the option from the menu you are given.

3. The board will now be viewable, and editable if you want, to other people. Sharing this board with all the others on your team will enable collaboration and accountability.

Trello is only one tool that will help you to create a Kanban board. You can also use the mobile app so that you will be able to keep up with your work on-the-go. However, there are a lot of other tools out there that can make a Kanban board so easy, and it's important that you try out as many as you can and pick the one that suits your needs.

Smartsheet

To start creating your first Kanban board using Smartsheet, you can start with the pre-built Kanban Sheet template.

1. Make sure that you are on the Home screen and then choose "Create New – Kanban Sheet."

2. Type in a name for your board and then select OK.

3. You can also choose "Now" to import any existing data into your Kanban board from Excel, Microsoft Project, Microsoft Excel, or Trello.

4. Your list of tasks will show up in the card view, which is one of four view types that you will find in Smartsheet. The other three are calendar, traditional grid, and Gantt. In card view, you will see four columns, which they call lanes, which are automatically labeled as: "Backlog, Planning, In Progress, and Complete." Now, you can add in the cards that you need for your tasks in the right lane.

5. Next, to add in your first card, select "+Add Card" in any of the columns on your board. You will get a form pop-up for you to edit in the information about your task, which

includes assigned to, priority, size, description, and title. You will also notice that the Status will automatically be listed as the land that you chose when you added in the card.

6. You also have the option to add in relevant documents or images, or you can add in comments to the card by selecting Add Discussion or Add Attachment.

7. Now select OK. The card will be placed directly into the correct lane.

8. Continue this process for all of the tasks that you need to add to your board. Make sure that you keep your WIP limit in mind when you start adding tasks to the "In Progress" column so that you don't become over-committed.

9. In order to edit your fields, you can select "Fields" in the upper right-hand corner.

10. Un-check any of the fields that you don't want to have shown on your card. You can also choose "Add New" to include extra fields in your card.

11. To create a high-level view of all of your cards, you can collapse your cards so that they only display the title of the tasks. This makes your board look cleaner. Select the icon located to the right of the "Fields" button to switch to a collapsed view of your cards.

12. Once a task is ready to change lanes, all you have to do is drag and drop the card to the lane it now needs to be in.

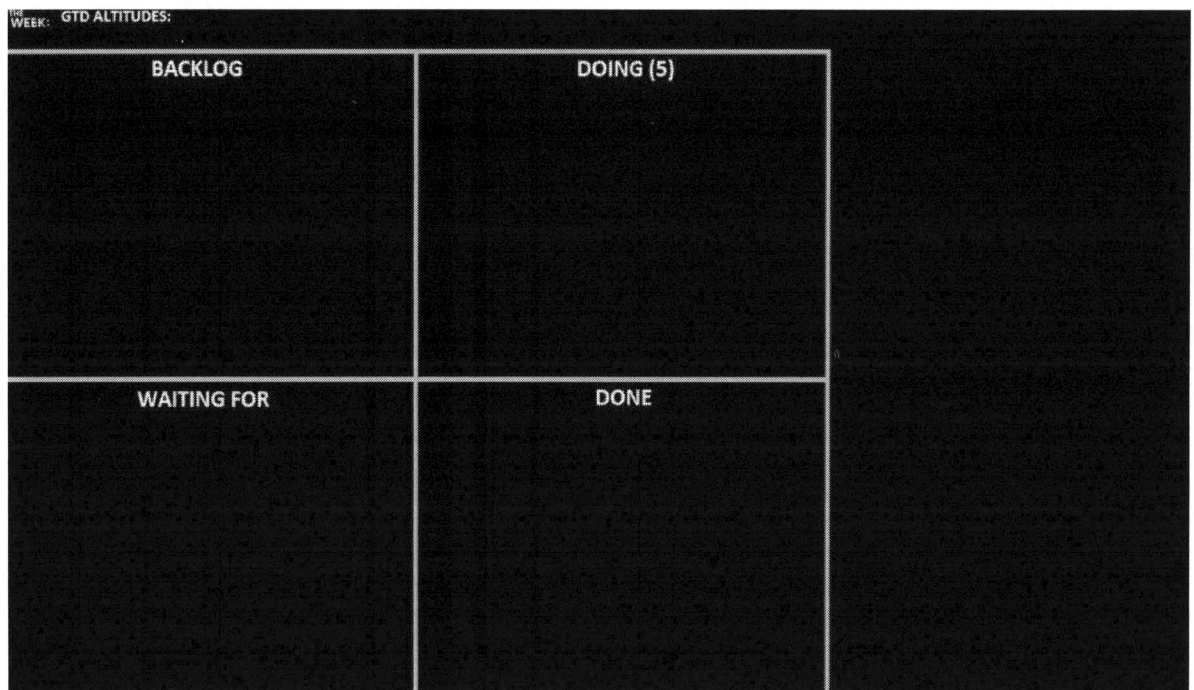

13. Any of your cards can be edited at any time by selecting the drop-down menu on the chosen task and then choose Edit.

14. You can now move through your stages of work and finish things up at your own pace. However, you need to make sure that you keep your Kanban workflow tenants in mind: don't breach your WIP limit, and only let the cards go from left to right.

15. An amazing feature of Smartsheet's Card View is being able to pivot your lanes. This is possible because you have at least two dropdown list fields for the cards, and will give you the chance to organize the lanes and see the work by criteria other than just looking at simply task stages.

16. By default, the template will organize the columns by Status, meaning start to finish.

17. Select the drop-down menu next to "View by Status" so that you can see the other options where you can sort your tasks.

18. By picking the "Size," the lanes will be organized by the size of the task instead of the status. This means that if you pivot your data, you can view through different criteria.

   a. Note: "View by" is unique for every user. This means that others that can see your sheet won't be impacted if you choose to view your tasks from a different value. Anybody that you choose to share the sheet with can view it through any setting they want without affecting anybody else.

19. Lanes can also be added to your board by choosing the "View by" menu and then choose "Edit Lanes."

20. Now, you can type in additional lanes that you want to add to your board.

21. To share your board, select the "Sharing" button. You will then be prompted to type in the emails of the people you want to share it with. You will then adjust the permissions to the right levels.

The best thing about using SmartSheets for a Kanban board is the ability to see the information on your board from different viewpoints. You can switch your view of your Smartsheet by switching between: grid, Gantt, calendar, and card.

Having this flexibility will make sure that even those people who aren't familiar with Kanban can gain some helpful insights into the work that is being done. Any changes that are made while in the other views will also be updated in the Card View. This means that your data will stay up-to-date.

Mapping the Value Stream

Before a Kanban is built, you have to come up with a value stream. Simply, a value stream is a list of steps that you need to take to make value. When you create a Kanban, the work will flow along the value stream, and this will help you to visualize the flow. This is basically going to help you come up with your Kanban board. You know how to create one, but you need to know how to come up with your tasks.

Before you get started, these are some things worth remembering about a value stream:

1. It needs to match up with actual reality as close as it can.

2. It needs to be only as detailed as needed so that you can see and understand the flow of work.

3. As contexts and understanding start to change, the value stream will as well.

Start with the End

What do you need to do?

If you are going to be in a meeting, you could:

- o Fully discuss a topic.

- o Create action items.

- o Plan a future task set.

If you are looking to get things done at home, you could:

- o Delegate chores.

- o Plan a vacation.

- o Build a porch.

If you are at work, you could:

- o Make important documents.

o Manage your staff.

o Build a new section of an airplane.

Every single example could have a completely different end-state. If you are coming up with a report, the end will likely be published. So if you were creating a value stream for creating that report, you would start with you "Backlog" and then end with "Publish." Everything in-between has yet to be figured out.

Fill In

Between your "Backlog" and "Publish" is creation. What steps do you need to take to create something? If you work backward from your endpoint of "Publish" you could have "Collation," before that could be "Final," before that could be "Second Draft," and before that could be "First Draft."

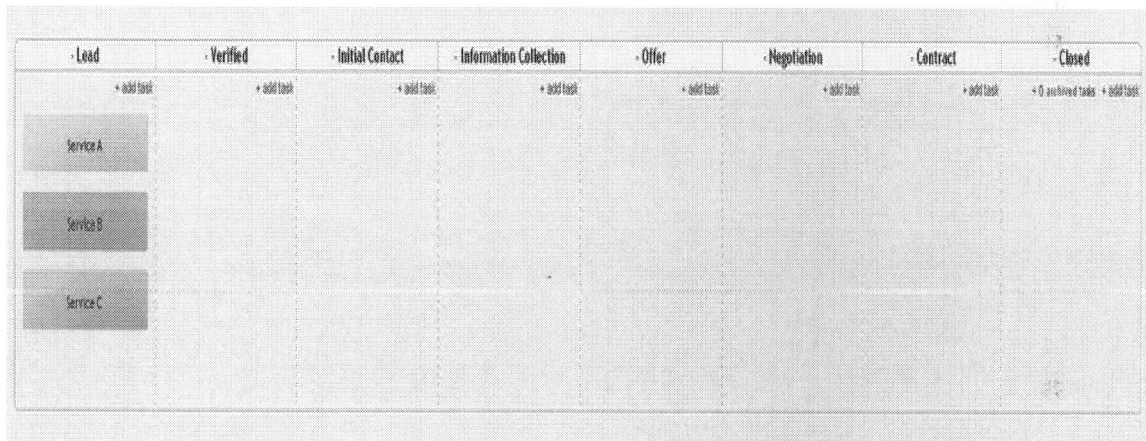

· Lead	· Verified	· Initial Contact	· Information Collection	· Offer	· Negotiation	· Contract	· Closed
+ add task	+ add task	+ add task	+ add task	+ add task	+ add task	+ add task	+ 0 archived tasks + add task
Service A							
Service B							
Service C							

This will now give you a stream where specific sections of your report can flow through. The team that is working on the report can track every section or chapter as it travels to completion.

Some important things for you to remember are:

1. The value stream is the best guess that you can come up with of how your work will actually occur.

2. The value stream is going to change.

3. The value stream is fault tolerant

Now, you know how to come up with your own value stream to add to your Kanban board.

Importance

Value stream mapping can be used to help improve the process of your work where you have repeatable steps, and especially if there is going to be several handoffs. The majority of waste in knowledge happens when there are handoffs between team members, not the actual steps. Inefficient handoffs might not appear as bottlenecks on the assembly line, but they can cause the same effect: less productivity, workers that are overwhelmed and lower quality. Mapping the process will help you to see where these handoffs happen so that you can figure out where wait times prevent work from moving along.

A lot like manufacturing, software development follows a process that is repeatable with distinctive handoffs, and continuous delivery is needed for the collaborative effort of the team.

Making sure that you have a clear and shared understanding of the process is important for software teams. Having a value stream mapping exercise for your team will reduce handoff delays, increase delivery speed, and improve communication. It will also help to solidify the process, making sure that they have a faster and more linear flow of value to the customer.

Kanban and Deadlines

A lot of teams that are adopting Kanban are coming from an Agile background. Thinking the Agile way discourages using Due Dates. This will in turn breed unwanted behavior. By focusing on Due Dates, it causes teams to work under extreme pressure. This will often translate into shortcuts being taken in the design and testing departments. The end result is that the quality of work gets compromised and then technical debt will pile up.

Even though project teams need to be self-driven and self-organizing, in actual reality, it could be very different. Not having Due Dates might cause momentum to be lost inside the team. This is when Parkinson Law comes into play. Scheduling five days of work could easily turn into seven days if there isn't any expectation set for a five-day deadline. If the project works on a fixed budget, slippage might pile up sooner than you think. This can cause an escalation of management.

There are many situations when using Due Dates at the task level would be very useful. The main one is not talking about resorting back to old ways. This will then cause the Due Date to become a deadline that is cast in stone. Then, the technical or quality debt would become a secondary consideration. It is a very useful guideline for a team member to see when they need to complete a task at hand.

So, you must be thinking how do I set a Due Date?

The normal approach is always estimation. Kanban systems don't use detailed estimations in actual hours but utilize story points. Sometimes, hour estimates actually exist. Projects done by IT companies are estimated by bids for the pre-sales lifecycle. These estimates are figured out by a developmental team. They don't often have the same set of details. Most pre-sale estimate gets expanded to better estimates when it is time to execute.

Using a Kanban system, sizing tee shirts is communicated by whether or not a certain card needs to be finished in one or two weeks. By doing this, teams can figure out the relationship between size and the time it is going to take them to make it. This will determine the Due Date.

The Kanban system also focuses on lead and cycle time data. It creates statistical charts that help the team make commitments at different levels like card, sprint, or release level. They can do this with an air of confidence. After figuring out the amount of data historically, teams that use Kanban can set Due Date to give guidance to the team members or show stakeholder and customers a timeline.

To sum it up, you must have balance. Agile teams don't like Due Dates since they send the wrong message and result in subversive quality and behavior. Having an absence of Due Dates might cause some teams to not finish their work. While Due Dates that are driven by estimates do work well, using a Kanban system can give additional assistance to teams to help them figure out better Due Dates. You can use Due Dates along with Kanban cards, but only use them as guidelines. Do not use it to make your team compromise the quality of the product or add to your technical debt.

The Seven Kanban Cadences

One of several things that show the difference between Kanban and Scrum is that Kanban uses cadences. A cadence can be defined as a rhythm of activity. An example would be to hold a meeting to plan once every two weeks. Then when the sprint has ended, hold a review meeting. Add in some more, you will soon feel the beat of consistent productivity.

Think about having no cadences, but you still need the meetings. Things will start to fall apart. You haven't held any meeting in months. You might decide that you need to have a meeting. Someone might come to you and tell you they don't have anything to do. Someone might ask you to do a meeting. All the meetings then start to feel like it is an emergency. This doesn't make anyone feel good.

Stand-up Meeting

This is the meeting that is held the most. It helps to keep the team informed about the project. It is used to address questions such as who needs help, are there any blocked tasks, who is working on what.

This meeting gives the team information to help them make decisions about what to do with their time. It is the feedback that the team needs and helps stakeholders in knowing what is happening and if they can help in any way.

It is held with everyone standing to keep the meeting short and sweet. The format of the meeting can change drastically. It can have a round of questions going from right to left and scanning the Kanban board to look for bottlenecks and blockers.

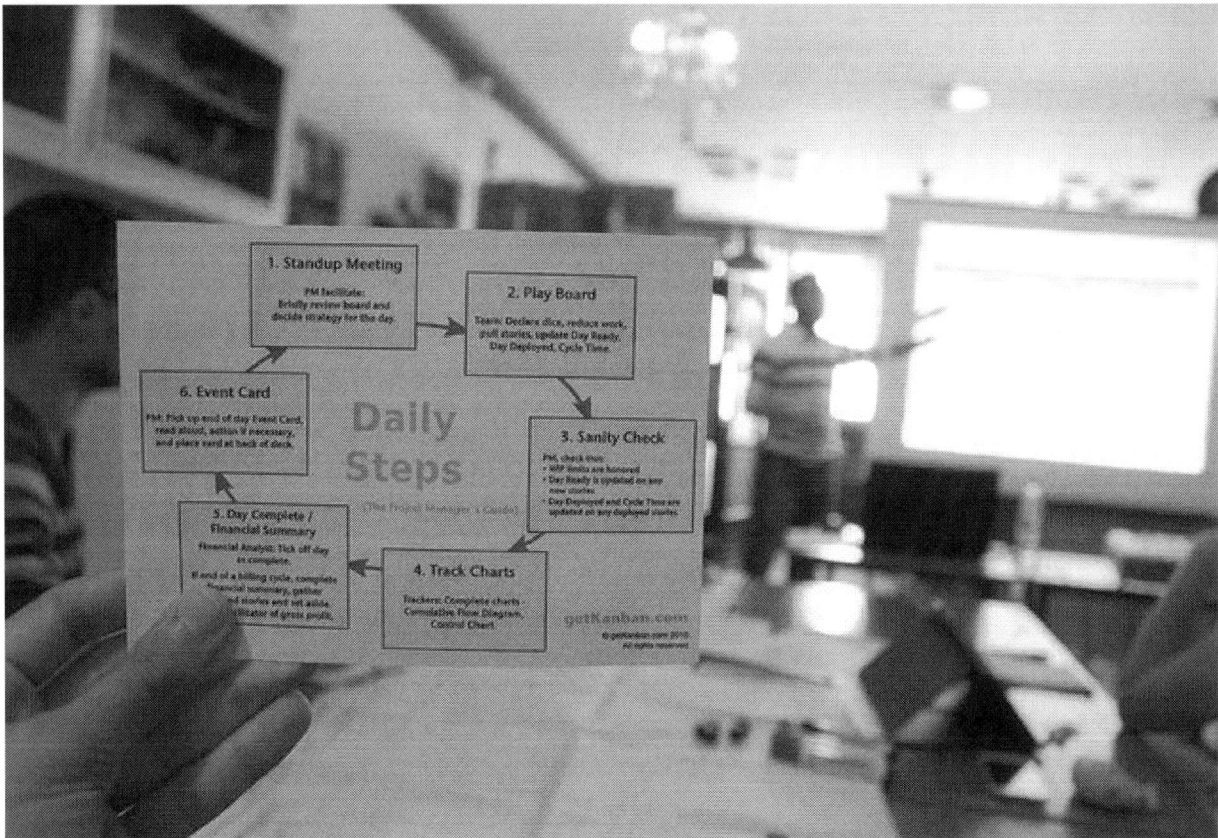

Replenishment Meeting

Systems need to have tasks in the input queue to keep from being starved. This meeting is when the team decides what those tasks will be. This is essentially a planning meeting. The format might be different, and the number of shareholders involved will change. If your team has problems prioritizing work that comes from multiple managers, you might think about organizing bi-weekly phone conferences with everyone involved to help prioritize the work.

This is when the word 'maybe' gets turned into 'should.' It is the step between possibilities and the company's commitment point. This is when the latest information is sent in. It is determined that a set of tasks are the most important thing to put into the system. If this is done frequently, it will help the stakeholders to trust that whatever is promised will get delivered regularly.

You just need to right people to be at the meeting to make the right decisions with the best data. This type of meeting can look different. It all depends on the context. You can have these daily or just once a year. It needs to be efficient in giving feedback and how quickly it delivers. You can even hold them on an as-needed basis.

Operations Review

This is a high-level view of how the different departments, divisions, teams, are working together as an organization.

You should know how bad local optimization is. You can't improve one part of the system without thinking about the other parts. One team can't save the entire organization if it has a poor delivery. Most inefficiency happens during handoffs and queues. During this meeting, different managers will find ways to help to improve the entire system.

By using input from other cadences, managers will see how the entire company is performing. Are the clients happy? Is the company profitable? Have there been many staff turnovers? Are there departments that aren't being used? Based on all this date, the team will experiment on how they can improve efficiency and lessen variation throughout the whole system.

Delivery Planning Meeting

This meeting shows if the company doesn't deliver right to the final customer. This meeting will smooth out tasks between departments or teams.

Customers might not want to see work piled on their doorstep randomly. They like being involved in figuring out when what, and how it is delivered.

Look over the output of stand-up meetings and the entire board of data. Look at any risks that might arise during risk assessment. See what is ready to deliver and what will be ready soon. This meeting will decide what tasks in progress need their priority changed. Tasks will be assigned a deadline, and the team might need to change their behavior accordingly.

Service Delivery Review

Are we serving our clients well? Service delivery reviews will look at the system from the beneficiaries' point of view.

Department and team efficiency will be wasted if a client is not satisfied. This review will explore customer satisfaction in all aspects of the process, how well the team's resources are utilized, efficiency, communication, and delivery. The main goal is improving customer satisfaction by building trust with transparency.

Look at the last batch of work that was delivered to the client. Were they satisfied with what was delivered, how quickly it was delivered, and how it was delivered? Were they satisfied with the use of resources that you had available? If things went wrong, were they happy with how you handled the problem?

Risk Review

This conversation could happen at all levels within the organization. It should happen at every level. It is needed to assess how likely it is you might fail to deliver, either to end users or downstream components.

Finding risks ahead of time and taking the steps to remove those risks will improve the system's predictability. This will, in turn, increase profitability and trust.

The basic level of risk review is examining past failures like rework, blocked tasks, and missed SLAs. It is also done by identifying the causes and finding ways to stop these from happening in the future. Comprehensive planning will include speculating about future risks by having them based on input and experience.

Strategy Review

This examines market changes and looks at whether your current goals are serving needs and being optimized.

Are you really efficient? Is it running like a fine-tuned, well-oiled, streamlined machine? Are you doing the right things? Has anything changed due to market decisions? This meeting should review your company's strategy and make sure you are delivering the value that will serve as your goal.

Compare recent delivery times with market trends. Did you deliver efficiently enough to adapt? If there are problems between your ability to make changes and the pace of the market, then you might need to change markets or find new ways to optimize your process. Company executives are the best to answer these questions. They have all the input from customer service, sales, and marketing. This meeting could result in new guidelines on how to evaluate products that are aligned with the market's expectations.

Time-based

These cadences need to occur every day, week, quarterly, or annually. This is good for situations where there will be value by having frequent updates or those important non-urgent things that may not happen any other way.

Event-driven

It isn't written anywhere that these have to happen at normal intervals. It makes sense to link some of them to events. Risk reviews should be done monthly. They might be triggered by bad failures. Service delivery reviews should only be done twice a year if everything is going well. One might be triggered by failing to meet SLAs in a crucial area. Replenishment meetings might be held each week or sooner if there aren't a certain number of items in the input queue.

Doing things well and finding ways to be better are fundamental to any work. You have probably already set aside some meetings that may serve all these purposes. The value of these cadences is finding out if you are getting everything done and evaluating if you have any gaps.

Analytics and Metrics

A Kanban system will give an organization several simple, yet powerful metrics that are directly connected to benefits for the business. When it comes to Kanban, metrics focus on looking on "time to market" or "time to value," and using these things to see continuous improvement.

CFD – Cumulative Flow Diagram

This is a simple metric that will give a lot of information about the team and system capability at a glance.

This is a time-based plot of your cards as they move through your board. CFD will start to plot the amount of cards that are located in every stage of your value stream. These CFDs are normally plotted every day, but for boards that move faster, they can be plotted every hour.

The different colors on the board indicate the different workflow stages. The band height at different areas indicates how many cards were in that stage at that particular point.

Día	In	En marcha	En espera	Out
martes | 01/02/2011	19	2	4	33
miércoles | 02/02/2011	19	2	4	33
jueves | 03/02/2011	19	2	4	33
viernes | 04/02/2011	18	2	4	33
lunes | 07/02/2011	19	1	3	33
martes | 08/02/2011	19	1	3	35
miércoles | 09/02/2011	19	1	3	35
jueves | 10/02/2011	20	1	3	35
viernes | 11/02/2011	20	1	2	38
lunes | 14/02/2011	14	1	2	28
martes | 15/02/2011	14	1	2	49
miércoles | 16/02/2011	14	1	2	49
jueves | 17/02/2011	14	1	2	46
viernes | 18/02/2011	14	1	2	49
lunes | 21/02/2011	14	1	2	49
martes | 22/02/2011	14	1	2	49
miércoles | 23/02/2011	14	1	2	49
jueves | 24/02/2011	14	1	2	49
viernes | 25/02/2011	14	1	2	49
lunes | 28/02/2011	14	1	2	49
martes | 01/03/2011	14	1	2	49
miércoles | 02/03/2011	14	1	2	49
jueves | 03/03/2011	14	1	2	49
viernes | 04/03/2011	14	1	2	49
lunes | 07/03/2011	14	1	2	49
martes | 08/03/2011	14	1	2	49
miércoles | 09/03/2011	14	1	2	49
jueves | 10/03/2011	14	1	2	49
viernes | 11/03/2011	14	1	2	49
lunes | 14/03/2011	14	1	2	49
martes | 15/03/2011	14	1	2	49
miércoles | 16/03/2011	14	1	2	49
jueves | 17/03/2011	14	1	2	49
viernes | 18/03/2011	14	1	2	49
lunes | 21/03/2011	14	1	2	49
martes | 22/03/2011	14	1	2	49
miércoles | 23/03/2011	14	1	2	49
jueves | 24/03/2011	14	1	2	49
viernes | 25/03/2011	14	1	2	49
lunes | 28/03/2011	14	1	2	49
martes | 29/03/2011	14	1	2	49

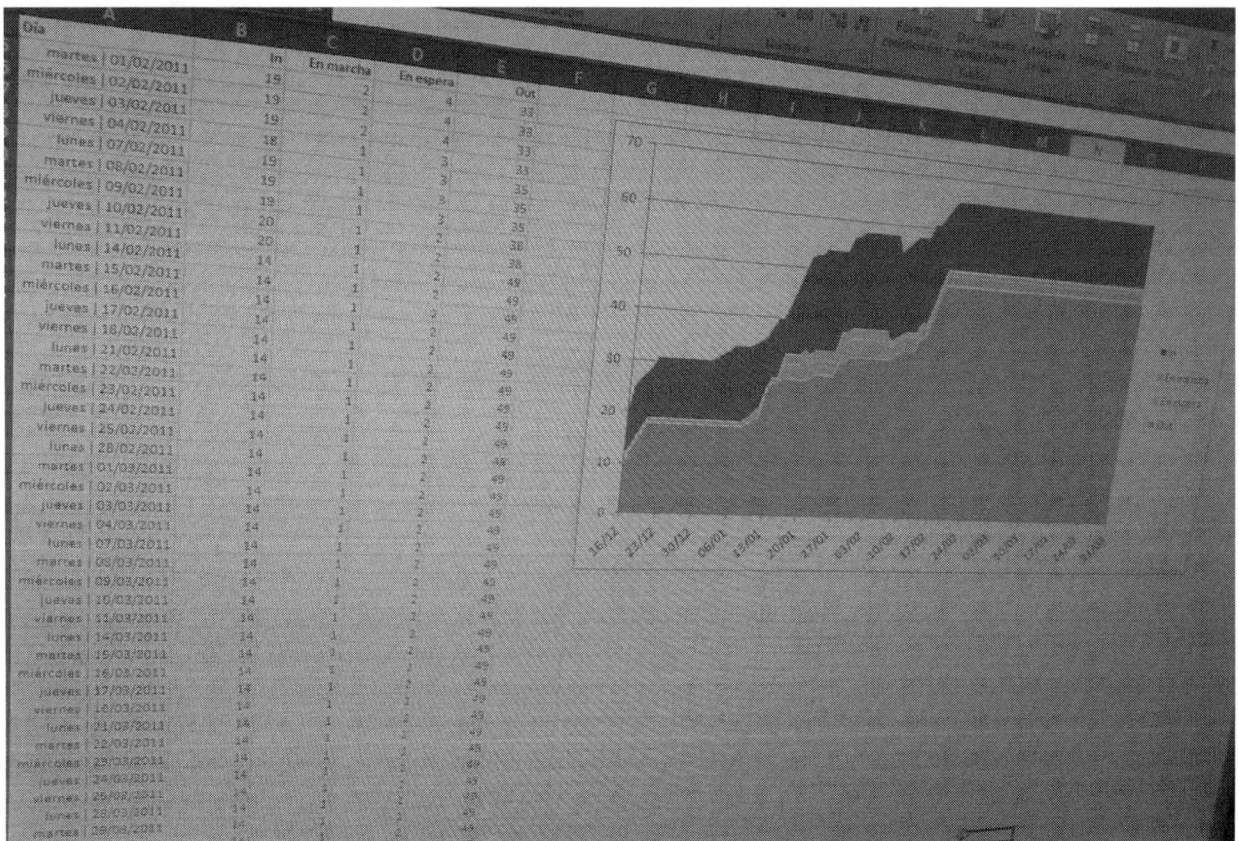

The top band is normally your backlog where your work starts out, and the bottom is typically the completed work. With an actual physical board, you could have a tray or envelope that you place the completed cards. For a virtual board, they are placed into an archived status.

As a whole, the CFD lets you know the number of cards that have been moved in and out of every stage per time unit and the number of cards that traversed the board. The CFD slop also lets you know how your system's throughput is. The greater the slope, the better the throughput, which means the amount of cards that were delivered per time unit.

A CFD is a great information source on how your team is performing and will provide you with information about lead time, WIP, and bottlenecks.

CFD gives you the most comprehensive picture of your system's delivery ability. Since the majority of teams work with lots of different items and have different experiences and skill sets in its people, the CFD provides a composite picture of what a certain team can do, and then you can use that info to predict what can be delivered.

Cycle Time Control

Every single process will vary. If you write your signature five times, they may look similar, but not two of them will be exactly the same. There will be an inherent variation, but it will vary between predictable limits. While you are writing you name, if somebody bumps you, you will end up with an unusual variation because of a special cause.

There isn't any common cause variation. Take a Tennis player for example. If she has great control, most of the serves will be where she wants them. There is going to be a slight variation, but not much. If she doesn't have any control, the serves will go all over the place, making more variation. With Kanban, there aren't any special causes such as wind, or change of ball. There are common cause variations. This will end up causing a loss in service and easy points for opponent, and could end up costing her the game, which is expensive. Likewise, with the majority of processes, reducing common cause variations will save you money.

Control charts will help you to see the variation. Control charts will provide you with:

  o Performance data plotted over time.

  o Lower and upper statistical control limits that show you the acceptable boundaries of variations. You will normally see these drawn at a distance of three sigma from the mean.

  o A center-line, which is usually the average of all the data plotted and is also called the mean.

Since data is typically distributed, the process is in control when 99.7% of the data is within the plus or minus 3-sigma limit. Whenever you get data points that fall outside of this limit, the analysis needs to be performed to figure out and get rid of the data because of special causes. Then, through further process improvements, you can also reduce common cause variation. This will lead to substantial benefits, especially when it comes to the system's or team's predictability and how it can make reliable commitments about the delivery of service.

Cycle or Lead Time Distribution

When you look at the lead time distribution chart, it provides you with how often cards are completed at different values of cycle or lead time.

Average Cycle Time Chart

This chart will provide you with exactly what the name implies, the average time of a cycle trend over a certain period. While having averages isn't the best way to come up with predictions about certain items or sets, it will serve to provide you with helpful insights of the trend over a certain time period.

When you look at one of these charts, you will easily be able to see whether the cycle time is going up, bad, or going down, good. When you use a combination of the three cycle time charts, you will be able to quickly catch these types of trends and make the adjustments that you need to, so that cycle time doesn't increase.

Cycle times of your cards are the total amount of time that the card will spend on the board, which is also the total work time and wait time.

Flow Efficiency Chart

This chart will highlight the critical impact of your system's wait stages. The majority of people won't realize that all of the value streams will have a number of wait stages. This could be handoffs between the different stages or the wait that is created by external resource needs.

Wait stages affect flow efficiency and cycle time. The bigger your wait times are, the lower your flow efficiency is going to be. Some of the best work teams that use a Kanban system will see a flow efficiency of 25 to 40 percent. This statistic means that around 60 to 85 percent of the time work is waiting for somebody to pull it, or for some form of input.

This measurement can be easily enabled in a Kanban system, and it gives you a lot of insight into your efficiency. It will help you to figure out how it can be improved.

Blocker Analysis Chart

When you use tools like WIP Limits, as well as visual cues like WIP Limit violations and Blockers, your system will highlight various impediments in the flow of your system. A blocker chart will help you to highlight a few of the root causes of the reason why cards are getting blocked, and you will be able to deal with these root causes.

The longer you cards stay blocked, the longer you cycle time will end up being and lower your efficiency. The analysis will help the team to figure out how to reduce blocking and better the flow and cycle time.

Throughput Chart

Throughput tells you how many cards are delivered during each time unit. This is a great chart to help you to understand the team's capabilities and make the best commitments to the customer about the amount of work that the team can provide in a certain amount of time.

Predictive Analytics

Overall, through using a Kanban system, you can easily and quickly come up with a graph of your team's performance data so that you can communicate clearly with your customers and the stakeholders that your system is demonstrating capabilities, and how you predict the future of delivery to look. You will also have an associated level of confidence and probability.

You can use an electronic Kanban tool like SwiftKanban to automate the collection of data and generate metrics. These types of advanced Kanban tools will provide you with predictive analytics capabilities using things like a Monte Carlo simulation to help further empower your team to make better decisions based upon the analysis of have you have previously performed.

WIP Limits

One property of Kanban, which is work-in-progress, is limited. A way to limit WIP is to match your team's capacity for development. You would normally set the WIP limit for each column or workflow stage. It is acceptable to set limits for each person or team. Setting a limit for any column doesn't mean you can't add another task in that particular column. Instead, it just means that when one limit is reached, the entire team needs to take responsibility and understand why this happened. They need to realize that they can improve and keep it from occurring again in the future.

WIP limits are important because they help improve throughput. They also reduce all the work that gets "nearly done." They force the person or team to stay focused on smaller tasks. Looking at WIP limits from a fundamental perspective encourages a "done" culture. WIP limits assure that bottlenecks and blockers are easier to see. Teams can work together around issues to understand them so they can resolve the problem that is causing the bottleneck. When the blocks are removed, work will start to flow once more. These benefits will bring value to the customers. Setting WIP limits is a great tool in development.

When you are in the development stage, it is easy to think about jumping from one task to another. When you are working on two problems at the same time, you have to switch between the two or transfer work to another teammate. Jumping from one issue to another is not free. It lessens focus and takes a lot of time. It is always better to work through one problem instead of starting and then not being able to complete a new task. WIP limits discourage people from getting in the way of their own flow.

WIP limits will show areas of overload or constant idleness. They will show the team their inefficiencies throughout the whole process instead of one area they work in.

When you set WIP limits, you need to ask two crucial questions:

1. How many people are on your team?

2. How many items can they work on at one time?

There are no secret formulas set for establishing WIP limits. It is normal that limits might be wrong, to begin with. You should never expect the limit to stay where you put it. They will need to be adjusted from time to time. You shouldn't stress over setting the initial limits.

Setting WIP limits will help your team focus on quality, completion, and making the right decisions. It also allows them to enable a pull model, get feedback to limit waste because of incorrect assumptions and rework, measure the number of tasks that could be done at one time, get a flow of work that will be delivered on time, avoid distraction by switching tasks and reduces multitasking.

Limiting WIP won't solve every problem your team might face. Not limiting WIP guarantees that you will fall victim to wasting time. If you don't have WIP limits, you will see that process improvements will be a lot slower. Teams that have used this from the start have seen growth and have delivered great results.

You can customize your Kanban board template by using Kanban Tool. To set up your WIP limits, go to "Setting," and then click "Board editor." Next, click the pencil icon in order to edit your WIP limit. Now all you have to do is fill in the "Task count limit."

Kanban Tool is an enterprising software that will allow real-time collaboration and allows you to boost your team's productivity.

Helpful Tips

Bottleneck

Has your team ever finished a project on time without paying any overtime or having any delays?

Bottlenecks are the main reason projects are delayed. Budgets are gone over because of the cost of delays, and the entire process has been turned into something unpredictable.

You don't have to fight the symptoms. All you need to do is an analysis and set up some prevention measures in order to save the process.

Use Kanban to help you analyze and identify process bottlenecks and figure out a flow that is predictable, and you will be in complete control.

The easiest way to define a bottleneck is, it's a stage of work that has more requests than what is possible to process at maximum capacity. This will create an interruption in the workflow and causes delays throughout the entire process.

Even if the work stage can operate at maximum capacity, there is no way to process all the work fast enough to get them to the next stage without creating any delays.

The bottleneck could be a certain department, person, computer, or the entire process. Normal bottlenecks are quality review and software testing.

The bad news is, most bottlenecks are only realized after a block in the workflow has been created.

There are effective but simple tools within Kanban that will help you spot a bottleneck and stop work congestion.

If you notice that your process often operates in bursts and has a tendency to be unpredictable instead of flowing smoothly, you will find a bottleneck somewhere within the system.

The main issue is finding it and figuring out a good countermeasure. There are several analysis tools within Kaban to help you find a bottleneck.

There are three easy steps to find a bottleneck:

The first one is to visualize. Keep track of work by using task cards on a board. This will show when work begins to pile up. This is the good indicator of a problem, which is usually a bottleneck.

The second one is to map out activities and queues. If you can separate activities and queues onto a Kanban board, you will be able to see how much time work has been waiting in queue before it moves into an activity. If this particular queue continues to grow faster than the work moves, you have a bottleneck.

The third way is to measure the cycle time within each stage. Measuring the cycle time of each stage will allow you to create a cycle time diagram. Just by looking at the diagram, it will show you where the cards are spending the majority of their time. Also, if these stages are in queue, you might have found your bottleneck.

What should you do in order to deal with bottlenecks? You should be able to resolve any bottleneck by putting more people or resources on a particular process or stage. This might mean hiring more quality assurance testers in order to get a better production flow.

What should you do if the bottleneck needs a scarce resource or an expert that is hard to come by? In many cases, these costs are just too high. But you should never leave a bottleneck untreated. This can cost you more money than fixing it.

There are ways you can contain the bottleneck:

You can't ever leave it alone. This will create a ripple effect that will disrupt the entire flow of the process. The bottleneck needs to be loaded at full capacity.

Try to alleviate the strain the bottleneck is causing. Work needs to arrive at the bottleneck in the best form possible. If the review itself is a bottleneck, make sure that quality control is done from the very beginning. The reviewed work needs to be flawless. Every error a reviewer finds will cost more money and time.

Manage limits within WIP. If there are liberal limits in the progress of the bottleneck and there is switching of context, you need to think about lowering the WIP limit. If the progress doesn't have a WIP limit, you might want to think about setting one.

Make batches of process work. The operation might take less time if you were to take time to organize similar work into batches. Be careful, because the bigger the batch, the larger the risk. The main rule is, smaller batches will always work better, but sometimes you must make compromises.

You might have to use more resources and people. If it is possible, you might think about increasing the bottleneck to help speed up the entire process. Just watch out. When resources within the system are distributed elsewhere, a different bottleneck might pop up somewhere else.

Seven Wastes of Lean

Getting rid of useless activities is extremely important for a successful company. This is a main component of Lean thinking, and it will help you increase your profits.

This idea originated from Taiichi Ohno. He ran the Toyota Production System and is thought of as the founding father of Lean manufacturing. His entire career was based on establishing an efficient and solid work process.

He found three roadblocks that can negatively influence work processes. These are Mura, or unevenness, Muri, or overburden, and Muda, or wasteful activities.

He figured out seven types of waste by using deep analysis. He called these the seven Mudas. They became a practice to help optimize resources and reduce costs.

What exactly is waste or Muda in Lean? Waste is an activity that uses resources but doesn't bring any value to the customer.

Activities that create values for customers are just a little portion of the entire process. This is the main reason businesses need to focus on getting rid of activities that are wasteful. By doing this, companies will be able to see ways to improve their complete performance.

An important note here: You can't get rid of every wasteful activity. Some are actually needed.

Software testing is not something that customers want to pay for. You might end up with a poor-quality product if you don't incorporate it. This will then have a bad impact on your performance financially. This creates two main types of waste:

Needed waste: This type of waste doesn't add value but is needed to do things in a timely manner. These activities could be reporting, planning, or testing.

Pure waste: This type of waste is not needed and doesn't add value. If something doesn't bring you value, it should be removed immediately. Any length of wait could be figured in as pure waste.

Getting rid of activities that are wasteful is critical if you want your company to have success. Waste can decrease how satisfied your employees are, decrease the quality of products, increase costs for customers, and lower your profits. You have to find the activities that don't add any value and fix the process where they are or get rid of them totally.

There are seven main areas in the Lean theory where you can find Muda activities, also known as the seven wastes of Lean.

Transportation waste is when you move materials or resources around, and it still doesn't add any value to your product. Moving materials excessively could cost your business a lot of money and damage the quality of your product. Sometimes, transportation might cause you to pay more for machinery, space, and time.

Too much inventory is usually the result of a business holding on to inventory "just in case" they might need it. Companies will sometimes have too much stock to try and meet the demand that they aren't expecting. They try to protect themselves from delays with production or possible low-quality production. These inventories usually won't meet the needs of customers and don't add any value to the company. They just depreciate costs and increase storage.

Motion waste is any type of moving of machinery or employees. These are both unnecessary and complicated. They might extend production time, and possibly cause injuries. The main goal is to do what you need to in order to create a process where workers don't have a complicated process to do their jobs.

Waiting is the easiest to recognize. Anytime tasks or goods aren't moving, waiting waste happens. You can identify it easily since time being lost is very easy to detect. Examples of waiting waste include: forms or documents waiting to be approved by supervisors, equipment needing to be fixed but sitting in the mechanic's shop, or goods needing to be delivered.

Overproduction turns to Muda when you have more merchandise than the customer is willing to buy. Producing more than the customer demands will lead to more cost. Overproduction will trigger the other wastes to happen. This is the main reason tasks or products are in need of more transportation, more motion, and longer wait times. If a defect happens during overproduction, this means your team has to work more units.

Overprocessing is a waste that reflects work which didn't bring more value or brought more value than was needed. These things could be adding more features to a product that no one will use. They just increase the cost for your business. If a computer software company creates apps or games that nobody knows how to play or wants to play, there is no value to that. They are just using resources and increasing the price of the computer. These are things consumers don't want to pay for.

Defects could cause employees to work more, or lead to scrap. Normally, defective work needs to go back through production, and this costs more time. In most cases, reworking of an area is needed and comes with the cost of tools and labor.

These seven types of waste can be very toxic to businesses. You can look at them as a way to improve processes and optimize resources. In every business, these forms of waste will have many different aspects.

Variability

A simple definition of variability is the lack of fixed pattern or consistency. It can be a liability to change or vary. Variability can cause more work and longer lead times. It can create a larger need for slack in resources that are not bottlenecked to help cope with the flow of work throughout the entire process. Variability within the size of the requirement and in how much effort is needed on delivery, integration, testing, coding, design, and analysis can affect the process and costs of running software development.

There are two types of variability: external and internal.

Internal sources are controlled by the operating system. These can also be called chance cause variations. Here, chance implies that the variation is random and the direct consequence of the process design. It doesn't say the randomness is distributed evenly. Changing the process design can affect the variations' shape, spread, and means of distribution. When we look at the name "chance cause", we can tell that while one certain cause might not be clear, a set of opportunities and causes to fix them already exist. An example of a chance cause variation could be the amount of bugs that get created on each line of code as required by each task or amount of time. The number, spread, and how the bug is distributed is affected by changing the process and tools, like doing unit tests, constant integration, and doing peer code reviews.

External sources are things that occur which the workers or supervisors can't control. These are also called assignable causes. External sources need different approaches in order to manage them. They aren't affected by policies, but you can put in place a process to handle them. This is usually handled by risk management. The word "assignable" means that a person or group of people should be able to find the problem and be able to describe it. These variations can't be controlled by a team but can be predicted. Plans can be made and processed, created to deal with them easily.

The main thing to remember is that the problem is easy to see, and action is taken to properly define the source.

Here are some internal sources of variability:

Since work items use stories or cases by decomposing the requirements, it creates the chance cause variation. Instead of using index cards to show requirements and increase the variation, changing the policy to follow a story structure can decrease time from five weeks to just one-and-a-half days.

It takes different amounts of time to complete different types of work. Measuring and managing completion of different-sized items can increase variability and reduces predictability. When you use techniques to find the work item types, you can change the spread and mean of variability and help the predictability for all types of work.

Class of service mix will manage service classes the same way work items do. You might incorporate a policy where these limits have to be strictly enforced, or choose to loosen up and allow an item to fill a slot for a certain date or time when there isn't enough demand for these items. You can switch the policies around during different times to help with the total economic outcome and make sure the system stays predictable.

Rework from either bugs being dealt with before its release or defects in production which displaces customer work will affect variability. If they happen during a predictable rate and are sized right, then the system can handle them. This is usually not the case. Rework that happens because of bugs increases the lead times, will increase the variation spread and reduces throughput. The best way to reduce variability because of defects is to pursue the highest quality with extremely low defects.

Irregular flow can be avoided by allowing time to complete most work. Irregular flow can be created by both external and internal sources. Predictability will breed trust.

When you can rigorously follow the different works in process, it will limit the randomness and classes of items of the different sizes and risk profiles. The larger the variability, the more you need to buffer. More buffering creates more work in process. The more work in process means it takes longer for work to flow through the system. This is the desired outcome since customers, managers, and owners value predictability more over chance.

Here are some external sources of variability:

These sources of variability are found in places that aren't controlled by software development or project management. These might happen due to server failures, power outages, other team members, or environmental outages.

Badly written requirements, vision, no strategic planning, badly defined business plans, or other information might cause a worker to be unable to make decisions so they can't complete their work. This item will become blocked because it is unable to make a decision. Now, new information is needed to fix the situation so the worker can make good decisions that will allow the work to flow to completion. Requirements ambiguity, just like other sources, can be influenced but never controlled.

Expedite requests are created due to external events like a customer order or because there was a breakdown in the company's internal process. Expediting in engineering is bad. It harms the predictability of requests. It can increase lead time and spreads the variability and reduces the throughput. Expediting is not desirable even when trying to generate value. Normally, within the Kanban system, expediting requests makes the delivery clear and will motivate the need to set strict limits. They need to be eliminated over time.

Environment availability is an assignable cause variation.

Some teams will see external sources as blockers. Relying on the environment and specialists like DBAs, deployment and system engineers are all blockers. Most organizations don't have any risk management capabilities.

There are two approaches to help reduce the irregularity that blocked items create:

    1. Define higher limits and accept longer lead times without predictability.

    2. Keep tight limits on work in process. Keep sizes low and resist longer lead times with lower predictability.

Doing and Done

An easy and simple improvement that you can make to your Kanban system is by separating states into "doing" and "done." This will give you a more accurate visualization of the actual state of a certain task. It adds a lot to the granularity of the metrics and is important to enable the move from a push to a pull mindset.

Let's say that a team has two columns: development and test. When a developer finishes the first story, they will push it into the test column. But the system is actually lying. Just because the developer has placed it into test, doesn't mean that the testing has started.

Now, consider that the development and test columns were both broken down into doing and done. Once the developer has finished the first story, they placed it into the done section of development. This will signal the testers that they can now pull the first story into the doing column of test. If large lists of tasks start to build up in the development, done column, then we can easily spot a bottleneck emerging in the before test. If, after some time, we notice that stories spend too much time in this column, it will trigger us to take a look into the root cause of this.

You could also choose to assign these names to the columns:

- Development
- Ready for Test
- Test
- Ready for Acceptance

The truth is that the difference is only intellectual. Aesthetically, doing and done is preferred, mainly because it provides less apparent states, and you can assign WIP limits in the doing and done column.

Conclusion

Thanks for making it through to the end of *Kanban*. I hope it was informative and able to provide you with all of the tools you need to achieve your goals, whatever they may be.

The next step is to start using the information you have learned. Kanban is a very helpful tool for everybody. It increases the efficiency of just about any task, so try it out to see if it works for your team. Whether you're a software developer or a project manager, Kanban can help.

If you found this individual book on Kanban useful in any way, can you please leave a review for it?

Thanks for your support!

Check out more books by James Edge

Printed in Great Britain
by Amazon